The Food Choice Jungle

The Food Choices

THE FOOD CHOICE JUNGLE

Christine Lewis, *B.Sc. Nutrition, London*

All food is for the stomach,
  but one food is better than another.
Ecclesiasticus 36:18
New English Bible Apocrypha

FABER AND FABER
London   Boston

First published in 1979
by Faber and Faber Limited
3 Queen Square London WC1N 3AU
Printed in Great Britain by
Latimer Trend & Company Ltd Plymouth
All rights reserved

British Library Cataloguing in Publication Data

Lewis, Christine
  The food choice jungle.
  1. Nutrition
  I. Title
  641.1   TX353

  ISBN 0–571–11424–5
  ISBN 0–571–11425–3

Contents

Contents

Acknowledgements

The author is indebted to The White Fish Authority, The Dairy Council, The Flour Advisory Bureau, Bird's Eye Foods and Van den Berghs for up-to-date information on food production; to Mac Fisheries, J. Sainsbury and Waitrose for insights into retailing; to Her Majesty's Stationery Office for permission to quote from charts in *Manual of Nutrition*, Ministry of Agriculture, Fisheries and Food, 1976, and *Recommended Intakes of Nutrients for the United Kingdom*, 1973; to John Murray Limited for permission to quote from a chart in *Success in Nutrition* by Magnus Pyke, 1975; and to the United States Government Printing Office for the United States Dietary Goals chart. Thanks are also due to her husband, Brian, and sons, Mark and Nicholas, for their help and encouragement during this project.

Preface

The Food Choice Jungle has been written in response to the questions people have asked me about nutrition. It is the result of studying nutrition formally for three years, talking about it professionally for five years, and practising it at home for a family for fourteen years. These years have been a time during which there have been great advances in nutrition knowledge and its application.

This book makes it possible for everyone to find out how food choice relates to health and wellbeing. Parents of young children will learn how to provide food for optimum health and begin good food habits that can last a lifetime. Homemakers of every kind will find shopping lists and menu planning less of a headache, learning how to balance the diet and the budget, providing better, tastier food, which often requires less cooking. Elderly people will find supermarkets less bewildering and will know which basic foods should always be in their shopping baskets.

For anyone studying home economics this will be a change from the formal books. I hope that students may accept this as a series of conversations about the relevance of nutrition, marketing, manufacturing and psychology to the ever-present work of choosing food.

CHRISTINE LEWIS

A Note About Metrication

Writing this book for the 'food chooser of any age' and writing at a time when metrication is taking place, I have been faced with a dilemma: whether to be completely modern and make everyone work hard with metric values, thereby excluding people who have grown up thinking in terms of calories and ounces, or whether to tell it all as I would to friends and acquaintances, using the familiar language of imperial values and adding metric conversions in most places. This I describe as a 'combination method'.

The exact imperial/metric equivalents are as follows:

$$1 \text{ ounce} = 28 \cdot 35 \text{ grams}$$
$$1 \text{ kilocalorie} = 4 \cdot 184 \text{ kilojoules}$$

For the purpose of this book the following table of equivalent weights has been used, thus avoiding the use of a multitude of small numbers.

1 oz	30 g	7 oz	200 g
2 oz	60 g	8 oz	225 g
3 oz	90 g	12 oz	340 g
4 oz	115 g	1 lb	450 g
5 oz	140 g	2 lb	900 g
6 oz	170 g		

Students will have more minutely accurate information available in the form of food tables. For them, in any case, this is a book of ideas rather than a textbook.

A Note About Metrication

PART ONE

1. Abundant Choice—Conflict and Dilemma

In the past, as in remote countries nowadays, women cooked for their families with far less concern than we do today. The limited range of foods they could grow, the comparatively few imports, the absence of recipe books and the infrequency of travel made for a simple life, and often a calmer and more satisfying one.

This book is for those who want to find their way through the present-day jungle of garden produce, fresh foods and manufactured foods, who are overawed by the number of recipes and the high expectations of the people around them, who want the confidence created by knowing that what they are giving their families is nutritionally sound, medically healthy, attractive and satisfying food.

Most people are finding the rising costs of food extremely difficult to cope with. Everyone has his own ideas about what to spend money on, but it is interesting to compare the relative costs of foods which are nutritionally equivalent and thus to consider the benefits of learning a bit more about nutrition. The result may well be less headaches in the supermarket and a more enjoyable time preparing, serving and eating meals.

The food choice jungle is a very dense one. Wives and mothers live in it always and many find it oppressive. They have a thousand meals to make each year! Our youngsters enter it unprepared and often curl up in a corner of it with a bun and a packet of crisps. Those living alone often find it almost impenetrable.

Many people have the responsibility of choosing food not only for themselves but on behalf of other people. Some have no choice at all about what they eat. For children it depends on the flexibility of their mother's approach. The Victorian attitude was 'Eat what is set before you', and in that situation the 'eater' was completely at the mercy of the 'chooser'. It is the same with some institutional catering today, so caterers are responsible for providing food which will foster good health as well as being enjoyable. A school caterer with only a hazy knowledge of food values may miss out some very important factors in the diet.

The influences which bear on our food choice are many. My own choice is influenced by a host of ideas, and some of them will conflict with others: as a housewife I am expected to bake the good old-fashioned recipes, such as stews with cheap cuts of meat, as well as being adventurous and cooking Italian, Portuguese, Chinese, Japanese and French dishes—and what a range of accessory ingredients we need! I am expected to produce a really glamorous and generous meat or fish course for a dinner party, while the children might eat low-protein canned meats. If I want to fulfil the 'image' I must make pastries like Louis XIV's French chef and sauces fit for Napoleon himself. I must make Cornish pasties for twenty, not because I am a Cornish farmer's wife with ten men to feed but because I have a freezer to stock up. Then there is Christmas, and I am expected to produce the sort of meal that was served in Edwardian households with at least four servants below stairs!

We are advised to cut down on carbohydrates, as we are overweight as a nation, and to watch the fat content of our diet because too many people are having heart and artery troubles. We are told that vegetarians are very healthy and wonder whether we ought to try meatless meals. Magazines explain how to make five-minute meals and fifteen-minute meals if the pressure of other work cuts down the time we have to spend in the kitchen. We would like to be considered discerning shoppers, gourmet cooks, lavish and loving providers. But we also admire balance and do not want to be over-preoccupied with food.

IMPROVED FOOD CHOICE CAN MEAN BETTER HEALTH

A varied diet is an excellent thing, and greatly to be recommended, but for some people the variety is chosen from a very limited range of foods. If these particular foods do not happen to cover the whole range of nutrients we need, our health can be badly affected. I hope to show how good food choice might improve many people's health.

If people understood more about nutrition, the doctors, dentists and nurses who spend so much time dealing with heart disease, thrombosis, varicose veins, obesity, gallstones, diabetes, anaemia in women, bad fractures in the elderly and cavities in children's teeth would be saved a lot of time. Their time, energy and money saved could be spent in research areas where resources are now restricted due to so much being spent on these preventable ailments. Chemists' shops would do less trade in do-it-yourself medicines, but their customers would have correspondingly more money to enjoy a wide range of luxury items.

Certain things tend to go wrong nutritionally:

Babies need a lot of protein and calcium. They are building up cells and tissues at a fantastic rate. Some mothers are keen to get their infants on to 'real food', just like the other members of the family, as soon as possible, and in such cases the babies may go short of the all-important milk which provides protein and calcium. Other mothers, who are keen to have 'bonny babies', may add extra dried milk to the formula for bottle feeding and thus overfeed. Such babies become overweight and stand a good chance of becoming fat children and adults..

Children and teenagers need more carbohydrate for energy. For children and teenagers protein and calcium continue to be important but their need for carbohydrate increases as more energy is used at these very active stages of life. Choosing the right foods for energy and in the right amounts is very important. Too much energy food causes overweight, too little or the wrong type of energy food makes youngsters droopy and lethargic. The eating habits which young people develop may greatly affect their adult lives, so it is vital to learn to choose food well. Surveys of what children actually eat have revealed some very curious and inadequate patterns.

Women and girls need extra iron. Through the whole of life vitamins and minerals are absolutely essential, but there are some danger times when the intake may be too low. The best-known mineral deficiency is iron-deficiency anaemia. Women and girls lose iron each month during menstruation, so they need more iron than men and boys do. The men and boys are nevertheless likely to get the larger portions of meat and extra eggs.

Older people need plenty of calcium together with vitamin D to protect their bones, otherwise brittleness may develop and lead to easily and badly broken limbs. *They may not get enough B vitamins,* and consequently feel overtired, edgy and lacking in appetite. They may prefer a cup of tea to a glass of milk, or they may cut down what they take in order to have a smaller milk bill. It might help them to discover how good some of the modern dried milks are. They may think that cheese does not 'agree with them', but perhaps they only use it as toasted cheese which makes it harder to digest. Some other serving suggestions would be helpful.

We all need fibre. One essential ingredient in our food is roughage or fibre, and this is often ignored. People used not to think about it at all. No one knew that in the body it turns to 'softage', providing bulk without calories and helping to prevent a number of illnesses. Where people are choosing white bread, white flour, refined cereals, cakes and a high intake of sugar, the importance of fibre has to be emphasized. One spin-off from changing to unrefined foods is that dental caries occurs much less in the teeth of children who do not eat white flour and sugar.

Many of us eat too much fat. The amount of fat people eat is another significant factor in their diet. Cutting down could bring benefits both for those with a tendency to overweight and for those who might have heart and artery troubles.

During the last twenty years there has been a tremendous upsurge of interest in food. The favourite topics have been delicious recipes and slimming. This is not a surprising partnership as deli-

cious recipes can make one fat and there is nothing like a slimming regime to concentrate the mind on the delicious recipes now
forbidden! But there is now a new topic of interest in connection
with food. That topic is health, and the interest in it does not lie
with cranks and hypochondriacs alone. The United States
Senate has taken so seriously the link between diet and health
that one of their select committees has worked to produce recom-
mendations entitled 'Dietary Goals for the United States'. The
aim of these goals is to help people to eat correctly and protect
themselves from serious illnesses. These 'Dietary Goals' are
shown on p. 29.

2. Value in Variety

It has been said that in the absence of any specialized knowledge about food values the best course is to select a varied diet, including some foods of all types, making up meals according to taste. This can work fairly well, but when we look at how choices are made and how many factors influence our decisions we may decide it is worth being better informed about nutrition. This chapter looks at what food actually does for us and the necessity of choosing well.

WHAT DOES FOOD DO?

The scientist shows that food, together with air and water, is the raw material by which we live. Our children's bodies only grow by taking in food and all living creatures waste away if they are deprived of it. The human body is a well-designed, well-balanced machine, capable of the most complex physical and chemical activities. This machine must be built, maintained, powered and protected, so our food must supply the ingredients needed for these processes.

UNDERSTANDING THE MAKE-UP OF THE BODY

What is the body made of?

All living things, both plant and animal, are made of chemicals and water, for that is what we find if we analyse body cells or the cells of foods.

When body tissues are viewed under the microscope, whether they be sections from skin, bone, muscle, kidney, liver or any other part of the anatomy, all are seen to be composed of a number of small units. These individual units are the cells. Cell types vary enormously between one sort of tissue and another, giving each kind of tissue its individual characteristics in terms of function, strength and colour. The picture below shows what you would expect to see looking at a piece of skin tissue under a microscope.

This is a cross-section view of cells. It's rather like cutting through a mountain of tiny bubbles, but in this case the 'bubbles' are cells, and they are not empty, but filled with minute structures and fluids, all made of chemicals.

Diagram Showing Cells in Skin

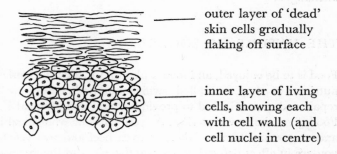

outer layer of 'dead' skin cells gradually flaking off surface

inner layer of living cells, showing each with cell walls (and cell nuclei in centre)

Notice that between the cells there is something else. It is a fluid, known as interstitial fluid, and this has the function of running a delivery service of food and oxygen, which it receives via the blood vessels, to the cells. It also has a waste-disposal function, taking away what is not needed and returning it to the blood vessels to be transported to the kidneys for excretion. Delicate chemical balances in this interstitial fluid are maintained correctly by the work of the blood capillaries, and in turn the interstitial fluid keeps the cells exactly as they should be, provided that we take the trouble to eat the foods we need to supply the basic ingredients. The messengers that ensure that the right supplies are sent to the correct place are the hormones. Within the cells the responsibility for taking in the right ingredients at the growth stage rests on the chromosomes and the genes within them.

The food we provide for our bodies, and therefore the food we make available to our cells, is taken in and oxidized (combined with oxygen) to make heat and energy. Some of the food substances are used to build and maintain cells, and the work involved in converting the food into exactly the ingredients required uses up some of the food energy too. The processes of making energy available, and synthesizing the materials needed for growth and maintenance of tissues, are known as *metabolism*. Living matter is not a definite substance. It is like a whirlpool constantly dragging things into its vortex and throwing them out again more or less changed while itself remaining apparently unchanged.

THE NATURE OF FOODS

Food is to be enjoyed, and food is also to provide the chemicals— nutrients as they are called—which our bodies need to build, repair and maintain and to provide mental and physical energy. Food gives the raw materials. As you eat your wholemeal bread and cheese and tomato salad, or roast beef and two vegetables, you are in effect delivering the raw materials to the factory, and it is important to make sure that none are missing.

In Western society we are basically able to buy what we need in the way of food; in other countries this is not so by any means. We may, however, be wrong in our assessment of what we need, or forget to buy something or find the cooking too much trouble and make an inadequate choice. Successful food choice depends on knowing the requirements of individuals. Everyone is different. Individual requirements change with age and type of occupation.

DO WE HAVE ANY NATURAL HELP IN CHOOSING?

Appetite might be thought to be a good guide to food choice—'A little of what you fancy does you good' and 'I know when I've had enough' are commonplace statements. But supposing that the poor unsuspecting appetite arrives at the worst kind of crazy, non-meal:

Soup: A broth which looks good and tastes good, but contains very little real food.

Main course: A pie whose meat content is suspiciously low. Overcooked vegetables, which were originally a good source of vitamins, but now less so.

Pudding: A 'chiffon' based on egg whites, sugar, synthetic cream, colouring and flavouring.

Now the appetite always knew where it stood with a bowl of homemade vegetable soup, brown bread and cheese and fresh fruit to follow. But its judgement comes under severe strain with a variety of manufactured foods. Appetite does seem to be a good guide where the food choice is from basic unrefined foods, but much modern food is almost over-appetizing and tempts us to eat too much or the wrong sort of things.

HOW ARE WE TO DECIDE WHAT TO CHOOSE?

The diagram overleaf sets out our needs very simply. It is not the complete picture by any means, but it does illustrate some of the basic things about food values and our sources of different nutrients.

One of the most important things to notice on this chart is that proteins, fats and oils, as well as carbohydrates, are all sources of energy. It is a myth that only carbohydrates can make one fat. Overeating from any of the groups of foods can create a weight problem. Energy is expressed in kilocalories (kcal), or, to be more

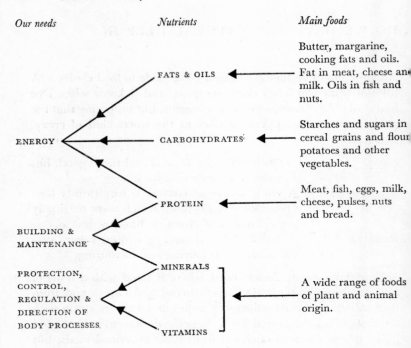

Our needs   *Nutrients*   *Main foods*

FATS & OILS — Butter, margarine, cooking fats and oils. Fat in meat, cheese and milk. Oils in fish and nuts.

CARBOHYDRATES — Starches and sugars in cereal grains and flour potatoes and other vegetables.

PROTEIN — Meat, fish, eggs, milk, cheese, pulses, nuts and bread.

ENERGY

BUILDING & MAINTENANCE

PROTECTION, CONTROL, REGULATION & DIRECTION OF BODY PROCESSES.

MINERALS
VITAMINS — A wide range of foods of plant and animal origin.

up-to-date, kilojoules (kJ). These terms are used to describe the amount of heat or energy which a portion of food can give us when it is metabolized by the body. (See p. 83 for further discussion of these terms.)

The diagram shows us *what* we need to eat, but the big question is *how much* of each group of foods do we need?

Our needs in terms of energy vary according to age, sex, height and weight, the temperature of our environment and how active we are. For example, a small middle-aged woman, leading a life of leisure in a warm climate, would need less food than most other people. Conversely, a heavyweight teenage boy doing a long climb on a really cold day in the Christmas holidays would qualify for very high-calorie meals. The amount of food we need for energy value depends firstly on our individual basal metabolic rate. This is determined by the amount of energy we use to maintain cellular activity (described on pp. 23–25) when we are resting and the basic processes of living are just ticking over. We need extra energy as soon as we take up any form of activity. Some activities consume much more energy than others. This chart gives estimates of how much energy food different people are likely to need daily:

		kcal	kJ
Man	Moderately active	3,000	12,600
Woman	Moderately active	2,200	9,200
Boy	9–12 years	2,500	10,500
	12–15 years	2,800	11,700
	15–18 years	3,000	12,600
Girl	9–12 years	2,300	9,600
	12–18 years	2,300	9,600
Child	3–5 years	1,600	6,720
	5–7 years	1,800	7,560
	7–9 years	2,100	8,820

These figures are averages and they represent people of average activity. If their jobs are sedentary, men may only need 2,600–2,700 kcal (10,900–11,300 kJ) per day. Conversely, farm workers and dockers may need 4,000 kcal (16,800 kJ) per day. Energy expenditures as high as 5,000 kcal (21,000 kJ) per day have been measured for jobs like woodcutting.

Weight for Weight Protein, Carbohydrate and Fat Supply Different Numbers of Calories

  30 g (about 1 oz) carbohydrate gives 112 kcal (470 kJ)
  30 g protein gives 120 kcal (504 kJ)
  30 g fat gives 270 kcal (1,130 kJ)

Beware of the double calorie value you get when you eat fat!
  Looking at these figures you have to bear in mind that many

foods contain a mixture of protein, carbohydrate and fat, so that their value as producers of energy (expressed in kilocalories) will depend upon the proportions in which these different factors are present.

Experts have suggested the following guidelines:

a. Protein in the diet should supply about 10 per cent of our calories and not more than 15 per cent. Normal patterns of British meals supply this amount.

b. Fat in the diet should supply not more than 30 per cent of our calories, and at least one-third of this should be poly-un-saturated fats and oils (see p. 71 for explanation of which foods contain these). In Western countries where food is plentiful people often eat enough fat to provide 40 per cent of their calories, so for most of us it would be prudent to cut down fat consumption by at least a quarter. Even then we are unlikely to be short of fats, and the amount needed to make food palatable is only about 20 per cent. This amount will also supply us with the other small dietary factors which fat brings to us along with calories.

c. Carbohydrates should be given a place of importance in our diet and should supply at least 50 per cent of our calories. These should come from cereal grain products including breads and from potatoes, other vegetables and fruit, which are all good sources of vitamins, minerals and fibre. In order to make room for these important foods we may need to cut back drastically our intake of sugar and sugar-containing foods.

The US Senate set up a select committee on Nutrition and Human Needs and their report was published in 1977. Much of what is true of the composition of the current American diet is true for the UK as well. Senator McGovern stated that 'our diets have changed radically during the last 50 years, with great and often very harmful effects to our health. These dietary changes represent as great a threat to public health as smoking. Too much fat, too much sugar and salt, can be and are linked directly to heart disease, cancer, obesity and stroke, among other killer diseases.' The report set out clear dietary goals.

US Dietary Goals

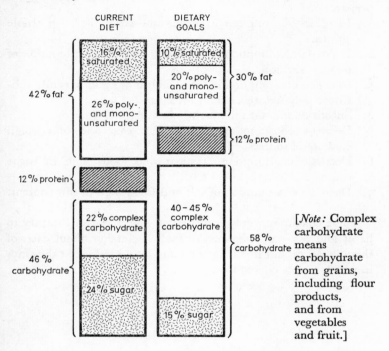

[*Note:* Complex carbohydrate means carbohydrate from grains, including flour products, and from vegetables and fruit.]

1. Increase carbohydrate consumption to account for 55 to 60 per cent of the energy (calorie) intake.
2. Reduce overall fat consumption from approximately 40 to 30 per cent of energy intake.
3. Reduce saturated fat consumption to account for about 10 per cent of total energy intake; and balance that with poly-unsaturated and mono-unsaturated fats, which should account for about 10 per cent of energy intake each.
4. Reduce cholesterol consumption to about 300 mg a day.
5. Reduce sugar consumption by about 40 per cent to account for about 15 per cent of total energy intake.
6. Reduce salt consumption by about 50 to 85 per cent to approximately 3 grams a day.

The goals suggest the following changes in food selection and preparation:

1. Increase consumption of fruits and vegetables and whole grains.
2. Decrease consumption of meat and increase consumption of poultry and fish.
3. Decrease consumption of foods high in fat and partially substitute poly-unsaturated fat for saturated fat.
4. Substitute non-fat milk for whole milk.
5. Decrease consumption of butterfat, eggs and other high cholesterol sources.
6. Decrease consumption of sugar and foods high in sugar content.
7. Decrease consumption of salt and foods high in salt content.

These conclusions may surprise you and may run contrary to habit and popular opinion. We shall be talking about each of them in detail, but first it may be interesting to look at the ways in which people choose food.

3. Making Choices

The average shopper may be influenced by shortage of time, a radio talk, a magazine article, the children's response to television advertising, her own weight problem, her husband's mood, the special promotions in the shops. Also by the likes and dislikes of members of her family, by social factors described as 'keeping up with the Joneses', and by psychological factors.

By contrast, the ideal shopper has a well-organized list based on nutritional knowledge. She has a schedule of well-balanced menus in mind and takes account of family preferences too. Feeling really fit and energetic, she is happily purchasing several days' food at once. Some of her criteria for food choice are:

—Does the overall choice provide balanced and attractive meals which suit the needs of the people concerned?
—Are the individual food items she chooses nutritionally worthwhile foods?
—Is the quality good?
—Is the price right?
—Does the list contain some foods which will make flexible meals to cater for latecomers or unexpected guests?

WHERE WE LIVE MAY INFLUENCE WHAT WE BUY

Part of our choice will depend on where we live. Traditions are very strong in different parts of the country, though supermarkets, freezer food centres and the big brand names have been trying to iron them out. Where we live may even influence how many meals we eat each day.

Food choice is related to the agricultural and industrial background of each area. This depends partly on climate and geology, as is seen in the marked differences between farming for food production in Scotland and in the south of England. In northern Scotland there is hill country and comparatively poor soil as well as a cooler and wetter climate, so rearing sheep and beef cattle makes more sense than growing fruit. In this region fewer people grow vegetables and fruit in their own gardens, and on farms the sturdy root crops (carrots, swedes and turnips) are more important than green vegetables. Oats, being a more weather-proof crop, are grown in the Highlands and wheat and rye in the Lowlands. So Scottish food tends to consist of soups and stews, using beef and lamb with root vegetables. Green vegetables are eaten less than in other parts of the country; there is less fruit and more baking, with oatmeal used for flapjacks and oatcakes. Porridge is a staple dish. Herrings and haddock are the traditional fish of Scottish waters. Kippered herrings and smoked haddock were developed as a way of preserving fish for times when the catches might be poor. Some of the remote islands have been very dependent on 'the boat', which called once or twice a week to deliver important foods like oranges. Winter gales could mean shortage of foods that most people take for granted.

Coming south to Yorkshire we find hearty English eating. Yorkshire people have a reputation for being excellent cooks, and the skills of home baking and preserving and the culinary arts in general are very much valued. At one time less cakes and pastries were 'shop-bought' there than anywhere else in England. More carbohydrate food may be eaten, mostly of the refined kind, and there can be as many as three main meals a day. Green vegetables and salads have in the past sometimes been neglected.

Industrial areas in the Midlands and in the north of England have been influenced more and sooner than other areas by wives having jobs outside the home. This has resulted in less time to spend on cooking because the cook is out all day. Fewer cookery books may be bought and food is chosen for simplicity of preparation, with many convenience foods.

In Wales, milk, cheese and butter are important foods together with Welsh lamb, all products of hill farming. The comparatively flat Caerphilly cheese is said to have its crusts just the right distance apart for a miner to hold a wedge in his dusty fingers during a lunch at the pit. The batch loaf is the same shape too. Stews, often called soups, are a cross between the two, with memories of making a little go a long way during hard times.

The Utopia of Country Cooking

It must be a nutritionist's dream to bring up a family in those fertile districts where rural communities enjoy an abundance of locally grown produce, sometimes even free of charge or exchanged on a barter basis. There are vast fruit-growing areas, people have great success with their own kitchen gardens, and there is plenty of commercial cultivation under glass to extend what is already a longer growing season than that enjoyed in other areas. The availability of fresh food, without having to pay for transport or receive goods which are several days old, is what is so desirable. With country milk and cheese, some homemade bread and home-grown vegetables and fruit one could be well content.

Supplies in the Cities

By contrast to these attractive rural areas, for the people of our towns and cities everything has to be imported from the country. For the big London markets, Nine Elms (fruit and vegetables), Smithfield (meat) and Billingsgate (fish), excellent transport systems have made possible daily deliveries of produce. The Londoner may in fact be in a better position for obtaining fresh food than the dweller in suburbia who has to wait for a further transportation of food out of London to supply the local shops. The Londoner has the widest variety of foods available in this country. The cosmopolitan nature of the big city (true also of other major cities) means that foreign foods and ingredients are sold in many shops.

THE POWER OF PSYCHOLOGICAL AND SOCIAL FORCES

Chief among the psychological and social forces affecting food choice must be the idea that a mother shows love for her family by feeding them well. Is it more loving to provide chocolate biscuits or oranges? It should be possible to combine kindness and nutrition, especially when there is an opportunity to put the new generation gently on the right track. Children welcome an opportunity to make a list of their favourite foods and they can be shown how to fit these into food schedules to achieve nutritional balance. This can be very important for young people growing up in an environment which contains so many attractive non-foods. If children are to have their favourite foods often, they have to learn to cooperate at other times when less favoured items appear.

Social eating, like social drinking, can lead to over-consuming. Badly balanced meals are often selected from restaurant menus. Diners taking too many calories and too much fat finish the outing with a headache, lassitude or gastric disturbance. 'Expense-account eaters' need to educate themselves about food choice. One major multi-national company gave the following motto for business entertaining: 'Frugality with dignity', and perhaps saved their executives from overweight as well as trimming the company's expenditure on food and drink.

We also need to consider the fact that snacks are often eaten for something to do, as part of an outing, or to show generosity. This can be a good thing occasionally but as a habit may not suit an individual's health.

Entertaining at home has been built up into an activity of great complexity. It takes courage to invite guests to join in a family meal instead of rolling out the red carpet, the best silver and all your most exotic dishes. Nevertheless, some people cook beautifully for 'company' and hardly at all for the family. A small child visiting our home once watched us laying a family meal and asked, 'Do children eat the same food as grown-ups?' Family meals are on the wane, with meals being requested at different hours and the inevitable intrusion of television. Eating together has always been such a focal point in the life of families in all countries and the major way of extending hospitality to friends. Surely we should not ignore this important aspect of life?

4. Protein is Pricey

To many people, large portions of meat served with vegetables once or twice a day are the only sure sign that they are being well fed. They are quick to condemn carbohydrate foods as fattening stodge, to be avoided by the health-conscious, and only eaten if people cannot afford 'better' foods. But, apart from being valuable as carbohydrate, many carbohydrate foods can also be considered useful sources of protein, for example breads, porridge and brown rice—although, as we shall see, the protein in these particular foods is best used in conjunction with the protein in other foods.

Protein *is* pricey when one thinks in terms of a meat-centred diet, with fish as an occasional alternative, but the budget can be considerably trimmed by bringing in vegetable protein foods. And provided that the foods are selected with care and blended into balanced meals, there is no need to think that by using vegetable proteins one is supplying 'second best' in terms of nutrition. It has been suggested that in future years we are going to resort more and more to vegetarian food, because plants remain our healthiest, largest and cheapest source of food. It is therefore time to learn more about vegetable proteins to enable us to choose wisely.

The following lists show which foods contain good quantities of protein and which others can make a significant contribution.

Protein-rich foods *of animal origin*	Eggs Milk Cheese Meat Fish

Protein-rich foods of vegetable origin	Dried peas
	Dried beans (soya beans best of all)
	Lentils
	Nuts
	Texturized vegetable protein
Foods containing a reasonable amount of protein, which should be used in conjunction with foods from the lists above	Oatmeal
	Wholewheat breakfast cereals
	Wholemeal bread
	Wholemeal pasta such as spaghetti, macaroni and lasagne
	Brown rice
	Green peas
	Broad beans
	Potatoes

Your choice of foods for protein will depend both on personal preference and on your budget, but you may find that some of the cheaper protein-rich foods can be very enjoyable once you have discovered really good ways of cooking them. Many of the best recipes come from other countries, where people have been more used to depending on vegetable protein. The cuisines of every nation reveal variety and interest in preparing mixed protein dishes. In order to reassure ourselves about the value of vegetable proteins it is useful to know about the nature of proteins and also to get a picture of how much protein different foods contain.

THE NATURE OF PROTEINS

Protein is a constituent of every living cell and proteins in food are the body's main building material. It is important to understand that protein is not a simple substance like sugar or starch, with a simple chemical formula. There are many different proteins and each can be divided into many component parts, called amino acids. A single molecule of protein may contain several hundred amino acids, linked together in a special way. Different amino acids may be represented by popper-type beads of different colours which can be linked in a chain. The number and type of amino acids present in the chain determine the specific nature of the protein. By moving some amino acids out of the chain and replacing them with others one type of protein can be changed to another.

After a meal, the process of digestion reduces the proteins eaten to amino acids, creating a 'pool' from which the body tissues can draw whatever is needed to build, repair or replace human tissue proteins.

We have proteins in all the cells of our bodies; particularly concentrated areas for protein are the heart, liver, kidneys, brain and muscles. Our tissue proteins are made from thirteen amino acids, and we must have foods which will provide a balanced mixture of these. By eating a mixture of proteins each day we can get the balance right. Of the thirteen amino acids, five are interchangeable, so that if there is insufficient of one type the body can change the amino acid chain to make the required sort of protein. On the other hand, eight are essential, which means that they have to be present in their own specific form and in the required amounts, and no substitute will do. Some foods will be especially good for some amino acids and short of others, but eggs, milk, cheese, meat and fish come nearer to matching human body protein in amino acid composition than other foods do. If we look in detail at the compositions of proteins what is interesting and important is that it is possible to use two or more proteins together in a meal to make up for each other's weaknesses. For example milk protein complements bread protein.

Many traditional British dishes combine animal and vegetable proteins, making it possible to use smaller quantities of meat per head.

Meal	*Ingredients containing protein*
Roast beef and Yorkshire pudding	Beef, flour, egg, milk
Lancashire potato pie	Meat, potatoes, flour in pastry
Steak and kidney pie	Meat, flour
Bacon and lentil hot pot	Bacon, lentils
Leek and bacon pie	Bacon, milk, egg, flour

Meal	*Ingredients containing protein*
Toad in the hole	Sausage, milk, egg, flour
Cornish pasties	Meat, potatoes, flour
Ploughman's lunch	Bread, cheese
Macaroni cheese	Macaroni, cheese, milk

Italian food follows the same pattern, using relatively large amounts of spaghetti, cannelloni, tagliatelle, lasagne and ravioli, made from flour and eggs, with relatively small amounts of meat, fish or cheese for the stuffings and sauces. These are good dishes to copy in the quest for less-expensive protein and are particularly valuable if wholemeal pasta is used. Sandwiches of meat, fish or cheese provide the same sort of combination.

PROTEIN IN NON-MEAT MEALS

An entirely non-meat diet can be adequate in protein provided that care is taken in mixing proteins. Then any shortages of amino acids in one type of protein can be supplemented by another. Two important amino acids which are especially significant in choosing vegetarian foods are isoleucine and lysine. Some plant proteins are low in these two factors, and as the body works on an 'all or none' basis in receiving amino acids it is important to make good the deficiencies in protein quality of any one meal. The following chart shows how some vegetable foods are deficient in isoleucine and lysine; also how other vegetable foods or small quantities of milk, cheese, eggs or fish can be skilfully chosen to balance with them.

Fish has been included in this chart because some vegetarians do eat fish while avoiding meat completely. For non-vegetarians small amounts of meat will supplement the vegetable proteins well. In any case, as most people are likely to eat some non-meat meals it is helpful for them to have some understanding of amino acid balance.

Foods containing protein	Poor sources of these amino acids	Good sources of these amino acids
Grains and cereals including bread, oats, rice, pasta and flour products	isoleucine, lysine	—
Nuts and seeds, except for Brazil nuts and sesame seeds (see below)	isoleucine, lysine	—
Legumes: peas, beans, lentils	—	isoleucine, lysine
Sesame seeds, Brazil nuts	—	isoleucine
Milk, cheese, yoghurt	—	lysine
Eggs	—	isoleucine, lysine
Fish	—	lysine

In order to make good use of vegetable proteins, while using relatively small quantities of animal proteins, or in some cases none at all, the following combinations can be recommended:

Using Grains

Oats:	Porridge with milk
Brown rice:	With curried eggs
	With fish as kedgeree or oriental dish
	With peas or lentils
	Vegetable risotto with grated cheese
Brown pasta:	With cheese, eggs or fish
	With lentils, onions, aubergines and tomatoes, as pastitsio

Wholefood and vegetarian cookbooks will help you to build up a repertoire of excellent dishes. This may include dishes using wholegrains like wheat and brown rice, nut roasts, and a variety of vegetable-based Indian meals. Well-chosen herbs and spices make all the difference to this sort of cookery. Other suitable recipes are listed at the end of this chapter.

Using Legumes
Peas, beans and lentils in their dried form are very important ingredients in wholly vegetarian meals, as are sesame seeds and Brazil nuts. You could use them in:

Rice dishes, as previously described
Thick soups, which are then served with bread to balance the protein
Bean casseroles
Bean salads
Lentil curries

Again, international cookery books will tell you how to make these meals really well.

A Note on Potatoes
Potatoes usually contribute some protein to the average diet, generally about 6 per cent. However, in some parts of the world potatoes are a very important source of protein and new varieties are being produced with a much higher protein content. Potatoes are deficient in an amino acid which is present in excellent amounts in eggs, so we could not make better use of potato protein than by serving savoury potato cakes, Spanish potato omelettes or jacket potatoes with poached eggs.

The two or three protein foods combined need not necessarily be in the same course. The most important thing is to choose good protein mixtures at each meal. The following meal, for example, provides a good protein mixture:

Pea soup made with milk
Rice and vegetable pilaff with toasted nuts
Fruit salad (no protein)

HOW MUCH PROTEIN DO PEOPLE NEED?

As we have seen, protein is a major constituent of our body cells, and protein foods are often described as building foods.

Obviously protein needs will be especially high when growth is taking place, as in the case of infants and children or expectant mothers. During breast-feeding too, when a woman is continually producing protein-rich milk for the infant, her own intake of protein must be higher than that of other women. In adults, the building usually takes the form of repair work, replacing worn-out cells on a maintenance basis. The only other time when protein requirements become greater for adults is following a surgical operation or physical injury.

Protein requirements are difficult to measure accurately for the following reasons:

a. They are related to body weight, but as each person's body chemistry is different we can only give an estimate requirement for someone of a specific weight.

b. The particular mixture of protein foods we eat each day is different so the total amino acid content will vary from day to day.

c. Individual foods each containing a certain amount of protein often have less than that in terms of 'usable' protein because of shortage of some amino acids. We can of course counteract this by choosing good protein mixtures.

d. Certain foods are more easily digested than others so that amino acids become more readily available.

In order to make sure that all these factors are allowed for, the United Kingdom Department of Health and Social Security recommendation is that 10 per cent of our calories should come from protein. Thus, for someone needing 2,500 kcal (10,500 kJ) of energy each day, 250 kcal (1,050 kJ) should come from protein, and as 4·1 kcal (17 kJ) of energy can be supplied by 1 g protein, about 60 g protein is recommended.

This figure of 10 per cent of calories in the form of protein is a convenient basis for planning meals, as it covers the requirements of young children and expectant mothers, but it is a high figure for adults. This explains how people in underdeveloped countries manage to live on far less protein than we do. The following are suggested minimum requirements:

—Infants need $9\frac{1}{2}$ per cent of their calories as protein during the first three months, then $7\frac{1}{2}$ and $6\frac{1}{2}$ per cent as they approach the age of one year.
—For one to nine years $6\frac{1}{2}$ per cent covers needs.
—For children over the age of nine the minimum requirement is $6\frac{1}{2}$ per cent, rising to $7\frac{1}{2}$ per cent by the age of fifteen, which means that it increases during the time of puberty and the last phase of rapid growth.
—For moderately active men and women $7\frac{1}{2}$ per cent is a figure which well covers the minimum requirements.
—For pregnancy and lactation the minimums are $7\frac{1}{2}$ and 8·1 per cent respectively.

Most British people eat 10–15 per cent of their calories as protein. Let us consider how this works out in practice.

If we take a figure of 60 g protein per head per day, this will be enough for women in the family and for girls up to eighteen. Boys from nine to eighteen will need 20–25 per cent more, and they are likely to get this by eating several extra slices of bread, more cheese, baked beans and larger portions of breakfast cereals with milk than other members of a family. One- to two-year-old children need only half of the 60 g. Two- to five-year-old children need about two-thirds. From five to eight years of age the requirement continues to rise towards 60 g. The 60 g is enough for men too because their minimum requirement is only 45 g. I therefore find that this is a reasonable basis for planning family meals.

One other thing to bear in mind is that for young children, taking lower amounts of protein, it is desirable that much of that protein should be in the form of milk, cheese and eggs so that amino acid deficiencies do not occur. Fish can also play an important part in children's meals, particularly in cases where milk is not tolerated or enjoyed in large amounts and of course meat is valuable too. The dairy produce items take first place in the list because they supply calcium (for bone-building) along with the protein.

Here are two examples of a day's protein foods each supplying nearly 60 g protein:

Example 1		*Example 2*	
*1 pint (600 ml) milk	18 g	½ pint (300 ml) milk	9 g
1 egg	7 g	2 oz (60 g) cooked meat	14 g
3 oz (90 g) portion of cooked lean meat or chicken	21 g	2 oz (60 g) beans or lentils (weighed before cooking)	12 g
4 slices wholemeal bread	10 g	2 oz (60 g) cheese	14 g
Portion of porridge or wholewheat breakfast cereal	3 g	6 oz (170 g) potatoes	3 g
		2 slices wholemeal bread	5 g
	59 g		57 g

* Adults, except for women during pregnancy and lactation, should use only half a pint of milk.

If these foods were being used for family meals, in Example 1 young children would take the whole of the milk and the egg but probably only 2 oz (60 g) of the meat and perhaps only half of the bread and cereal. Thus their total protein intake would be about 50 g and they would be getting their full requirements of animal protein foods. Other food portions which might be chosen are 3 oz (90 g) cooked white fish (15 g protein), 2 wholewheat breakfast cereal biscuits (4 g protein) or 1 oz (30 g) roasted peanuts (8 g protein).

We tend to think of protein foods being catered for in the main course only, but a dessert may contribute quite a lot of protein. Examples are egg custard, bread and butter pudding, Bakewell tart, cheesecake, pancakes and rice pudding. If the main course is vegetable-based rather than meat-based on some days, puddings like these can make a valuable contribution to the total protein intake. It is also worth noting how useful a glass of milk can be when served with a simple meal.

ADVANTAGES OF USING MORE VEGETABLE PROTEIN

There is quite a lot of prejudice against plant protein in the wealthier countries. The ability to provide good meat meals has been such an important status symbol. Lentil stews and pease puddings have been associated with hard times and years of economic depression. The use of brown rice and nuts has been linked with 'cranky' attitudes and vegetarianism has only recently come to enjoy a more favourable image. Perhaps this is because there are now seen to be good reasons for using at least some vegetable protein.

The Price is Right

For those who are working to a fairly tight budget the cost of serving a meal based on beans or lentils will be one-half to one-third of that of a meal based on meat.

The Total Fat in the Meal is Reduced

If you are concerned to eat less saturated fats and cholesterol, vegetable proteins can help you. There is little or no fat in grains and pulses, polyunsaturated fats only in most nuts and seeds and no cholesterol in any of them (terms explained on pp. 71 and 73). Saturated fats are potential trouble-makers for those with a tendency to heart and artery trouble, and the fat in meat is mainly of this type. It is possible to cut off the visible fat but meat always contains 'hidden' fat as well. Even lean meat is often marbled with streaks of fat; in fact butchers make a feature of well-marbled joints of beef because they are known to make the most tender roasts and grills. It used to be customary to lard beef by threading strips of lard through the lean flesh to improve the quality of the meat.

Because of the amount of fat in meat it is prudent to serve small portions, and to beware of the lavish sauces sometimes provided which encourage the diner to eat more meat than his appetite would normally dictate. An alternative is to use vegetable proteins as meat 'extenders', enabling small quantities of meat to be enjoyed and keeping the protein value of the meal high enough. Or we may choose some all-vegetable meals, as have been previously described.

The Fibre Content of the Meal is Improved

Beans, peas and lentils are fibre-rich foods, and in recent years it has been shown that people are healthier if their meals contain sufficient fibre. This comes from plant sources and so from the vegetable part of our diet. Besides the pulses mentioned above, everything made from cereal grains which have not had the outer brown layer removed is full-fibre food. The list includes porridge oats, wholewheat flour, breads, biscuits and breakfast cereals, brown rice and brown pasta. Everything mentioned in this section is brown as opposed to white, that is, unrefined as opposed to refined. Much of our present-day food has been fibre-depleted by modern processing methods. (See next chapter for more on fibre.)

It is interesting and helpful when studying nutrition to see how some foods which are good for their contribution of one nutrient, for example protein, actually 'match' with a list of foods rich in another necessary factor, in this case fibre. As we continue to think about food values, in particular when we consider vitamins and minerals, other 'matching' will be noticed. Gradually a picture will be built up showing ways of choosing foods which have many uses. It is like hiring versatile staff!

Vegetable Protein is More Economical to Produce

In the natural world, plants are the manufacturers of protein, which they make from basic ingredients: water, carbon dioxide and nitrogen. So plants are the primary source of protein and animals and humans must eat plant protein to live. Plant protein may be consumed as plant material, which happens when cows eat grass and when we eat beans and bread. Alternatively, plant protein eaten by one animal is converted into animal protein, subsequently to be eaten by other animals or by humans.

When cattle are reared for milk production one-fifth of the plant protein fed to the cattle finally appears as milk protein. If beef is produced one-tenth of the plant protein appears as meat protein. In both cases there is a high degree of wastage and a great deal of expense. If countries are short of protein it makes good sense to consume more vegetable and less animal protein. Sadly, the vegetable-based cattle feedstuffs which we import are often from countries where that food could well be used as vegetable protein for humans.

THE IMPORTANCE OF EATING CARBOHYDRATE WITH PROTEIN

The protein in vegetable foods is always associated with a quantity of starch, providing carbohydrate for energy at the same time as protein for building and repair. In animal protein foods there is no carbohydrate, the associated nutrient being fat, so carbohydrate to eat with the protein must be supplied in the form of potatoes, bread, rice or pasta. Alternatively, a pastry crust or a Yorkshire pudding or perhaps a pudding or pie for dessert will add carbohydrate.

The importance of taking carbohydrate with protein stems from the following facts. The body uses energy for the processes of metabolizing food, and more energy is required for dealing with protein than for either carbohydrate or fat. This energy can be supplied by carbohydrate calories, from fat calories, or from the calories of other protein, but protein is wasted if it is used just to provide energy when it is capable of the nobler activity of actually providing building material. It is like taking expensive seasoned wood and burning it to keep the carpenters warm.

Provided that carbohydrate is present in each meal the protein is spared for its major work.

As energy is used in metabolizing food after a meal, heat production in the body increases, and this is particularly so after large meals of concentrated protein taken in a hot climate or a warm room. Diners may feel uncomfortably hot after a menu of seafood, steak and a choice of cheeses. Conversely, it is important for elderly people who feel the cold to have enough protein, in winter especially, in order to keep up this heat-producing activity within the body.

THE COST OF PROTEIN FOODS

If we set out to buy protein foods thinking about cost alone our money would be best spent on the following foods. (In these lists the foods that are the cheapest sources of protein appear at the top of each list.)

Soya beans	Milk
Split peas	Cheese
Haricot and other beans	Eggs
Lentils	
Peanuts and almonds	
Bread, wholemeal preferably	
Oatmeal	

Dishes based on mixtures of these foods would give variety and satisfy our protein needs.

Still aiming to keep costs low we might add:

Wholegrain breakfast cereals	Herrings
Potatoes	Minced mutton
Frozen or fresh peas	Liver
	Chicken
	Streaky bacon
	Belly of pork
	Stewing beef
	Sausages

If there is more money available we could buy:

Cod   Beef
Coley   Bacon
Lamb   Turkey
Pork

And if money is no object:

Fillet steak   Sole
Salmon   Fancy cheeses
Shellfish

How to Save Money When Buying Protein Foods

Meat and fish. The cuts and varieties chosen make a great difference to the price, but weight for weight lean stewing beef can give
the same amount of protein as grilling steak, and the same is true
of fish in different price ranges. The way we cook meat affects the
extent to which the body can use the protein. Medium-done
roasts and grills and slowly cooked casseroles or stews all fulfil the
objective of increasing protein digestibility.

Milk. Skimmed milk powder makes up to a milk of equivalent
protein value to fresh milk and costs less. Provided that it is not
used for infant feeding it is an acceptable substitute for fresh
milk.

Cheese. This varies in protein content according to the variety
chosen. The English and Dutch firm cheeses give good protein
value, with Cheddar the cheapest, followed by Cheshire. Cream
cheeses and cheese spreads may be quite low in protein, and
should not be thought of as reliable sources of building foods.
Some may be quite good, others very poor in protein. Note that
cheese spreads are always highly priced compared with hard
cheeses.

Eggs. Prices fluctuate seasonally. White eggs are usually cheaper
but have the same protein value as brown eggs. Small or medium
eggs (sizes 5 or 6) work out cheaper by weight if they are more
than 5p per dozen less than sizes 3 or 4.

Egg protein is nearer to human protein in amino acid content than any other protein. It is not deficient in any of the amino acids which we need and even has an excess of some of them, which makes it very useful in complementing other protein foods. For example, in Chinese cooking, eggs are used in small quantities in Chow Mein, egg flower soup and small omelettes which are sliced and arranged over vegetable dishes.

Beans, split peas and lentils. These cost more when bought in small packets from grocery stores than if purchased from a health food or Asian food store where people customarily buy pulses in large quantities and often at a discount. All these items store well, so bulk purchases can be made quite safely. The cheaper of these pulses are Aduki beans, yellow split peas, chick peas and soya beans. Then come Mung beans (generally used for sprouting), split green beans and green lentils. Finally, black-eyed beans, red lentils, red wonder beans, butter beans and haricot beans cost more than the others.

Pulses should be boiled for five minutes and then left to soak in the water for one hour before cooking. This softens them quickly and is better than the overnight soaking usually recommended. Pressure cooking cuts down on the long cooking time, saves fuel costs and conserves food value. To give some idea of the quantities used, one generally allows 2 oz (60 g) dried pulses per head for a main course dish and 1–1½ oz (30–45 g) per head for a soup. A list of recipes at the end of this chapter is intended as a guide to searching out good bean and lentil recipes in international cookbooks.

Nuts. The highest protein value is found in peanuts. Almonds come next, then Brazils and walnuts, which have about half the protein value of peanuts. Hazelnuts follow with a slightly lower value still. Peanuts are always the cheapest as well as the best source of nut protein. (This means plain peanuts, not roasted in oil and salt, but used in salads, nut roasts and risottos.) All nuts can be purchased in their shells, but they are a seasonal commodity, and in general the cost of buying them ready-shelled is no greater. Some chain supermarkets sell nuts cheaper than health food shops do. Blanched and skinned nuts are considerably more expensive than unprocessed nuts. Ground almonds particularly cost quite a lot more and are worth preparing at home if one has a liquidizer-grinder or hand-operated mill. Remember that nuts need to be combined with other protein foods to compensate for their amino acid deficiency.

Bread. It has been rightly said that a diet including a lot of wholemeal bread is likely to be adequate in total protein, particularly if it also includes some milk, cheese and eggs. Wholemeal bread, homemade from 100 per cent wholemeal flour and dried yeast (for convenience) costs only two-thirds as much as shop-bought wholemeal bread. If the shop makes only small loaves your homemade bread will cost only half as much, as we always pay more for smaller loaves. Brown bread can be regarded as a staple food for protein; it is satisfying and people do not usually eat too much of it as they often do with white bread.

Oatmeal. It is useful to look out the best Scottish recipes for porridge, oatcakes, mince collops, parkin and various biscuits, and then to decide which types of oatmeal to stock. I personally keep rolled oats for the morning porridge and for biscuit-making, together with a medium-grain oatmeal for adding to minced beef, for making oatcakes and patties, and for coating herrings and mackerel before cooking. The rolled oats come in 7 lb bags from a deep-freeze centre, the medium oatmeal from a wholefood store.

Brown rice. This has a higher protein value than white rice. It costs more, so you will not save money by buying it, but for protein, vitamins and fibre it makes very good sense to choose it.

Texturized vegetable protein—TVP. Many people do not know what texturized vegetable protein really is. The protein part is in fact likely to come from soya beans, which of all vegetable foods have the best protein value. 'Texturizing' refers to the way the protein is given a fibrous texture so that it looks and 'chews' very much like meat. It is then either made into chunks for stews and casseroles or minced. The fact that the texturizing process was designed by a manufacturer of fabric textiles puts some people off trying TVP, but nutritionally speaking it is a real food. The advantages of using vegetable proteins have already been discussed (see pp. 45–7). 5 oz (140 g) TVP makes up to 1 lb (450 g) meat substitute after rehydrating (water is added and the TVP is simmered for two to three minutes).

Soya protein has been used in manufactured foods for many years. Long before anyone thought of texturizing it, soya flour was used by bakers to replace non-fat dried milk in cakes, doughnuts and biscuits and in cake and pancake mixes. It is also widely used in high-protein breads and biscuits and has been added to some breakfast cereals to improve the amino acid balance. Some sausages, pies and patties also contain soya protein.

As texturized vegetable protein, soya can be made to simulate ham cubes, pieces of chicken or bacon, or minced or stewing beef, but to achieve this variety all kinds of flavourings have to be added and it is this aspect that discourages me from choosing TVP often.

When TVP is used on its own the flavour is not the same as that of meat. So it is best used in highly flavoured dishes such as curries or chilli con carne—or chilli con TVP! The other main use is as a meat-extender added to minced beef to give more meat at lower cost. There is a natural-flavoured TVP which is good for this purpose.

Processing soya protein is not an entirely new concept. Chinese and Japanese people have traditionally used vegetable proteins from soya, rice and barley to provide 90 per cent of their total protein. The time-honoured ways of preparing protein-rich foods from soya beans are as soya bean milk, soya cheese (*natto*), soya curds (*tofu*), high-protein sticks (*yuba*), and sheets or flakes made by boiling soya bean milk and collecting the surface film. Soya beans are also widely used in their own right as vegetables.

In the USA there has been a great deal of interest in the development of TVP for main meals. This has been linked with a demand for health foods and lower fat content in foods, and also with many people's religious scruples against the use of meat. It has become commonplace for hamburgers to have up to 30 per cent soya protein, and there is authorization for 30 per cent of the meat in the school lunch programme to be replaced by soya protein. Gradually TVP is also being successfully introduced into institutional catering in Britain.

LIST OF INTERNATIONAL RECIPES TO SEEK
OUT FOR REALLY ENJOYING DRIED PEAS
AND BEANS

English:	Pease pudding
American:	Boston baked beans
	Black-eyed beans with pork
French:	Cassoulet
Italian:	Venetian bean soup
	Piedmont bean and bacon stew
Spanish:	Kidney beans and rice in tomato sauce
	Omelette with peas and potatoes
Swedish:	Yellow pea soup
Mexican:	Chilli con carne
Cuban:	Moors and Christians, a dish of black and white beans
Japanese:	Aduki beans and rice
Egyptian:	Brown beans with sliced hard-boiled eggs
Greek:	Hummus, made with chick peas

Some bean salads
Red bean salad
Tuna and haricot bean salad
Multi-coloured bean salad

5. The Case for Carbohydrates

The case against carbohydrates has been put strongly for many years. Ask for a quick verdict on carbohydrate and the answer is likely to be, 'Bread, potatoes, sugar, all the fattening things.' Carbohydrates have in many people's minds become the enemy of slimness and fitness, the big temptation, the addiction which comes between them and next year's bikini. This is a very narrow view and one that is hard to reconcile with the recommendation that *for good health our diet should contain 40–45 per cent complex carbohydrate* (that is, carbohydrate derived from grains including flour and breakfast cereals, vegetables and fruit) *and not more than 15 per cent sugar*, derived from the naturally-occurring sugars in fruit, cane and beet sugars, syrups and honey.

The answer is that if most of our carbohydrate comes from refined foods, and our liking for sweet things is pronounced, our carbohydrate intake may be too great and of the wrong kind. On the other hand, when much of our carbohydrate comes from wholegrain cereals, vegetables and fruit we can safely eat quite a lot of carbohydrate and it will suit our metabolism very well indeed. Carbohydrate foods should be an important and delicious part of our meals and not just guilt-complex producers.

THE NATURE OF CARBOHYDRATES

Carbohydrates are the nutrients made up of *sugars, starches* (which are actually broken down into sugars as they are digested) and *celluloses* (now described as *fibre*). Sugars and starches are energy-producing nutrients. Celluloses are responsible for the structure of plants and their value to us is that they provide fibre.

Most foods contain a mixture of nutrients. Apart from sugar, which is carbohydrate and nothing else, all the other foods roughly described as carbohydrate foods in fact also contain other nutrients.

STARCHES

These are mixtures of substances and contain large numbers of glucose molecules (sugars) which are released from food for the body's use by the process of digestion.

Where do starches come from? One well-known source is grains, another is vegetables which grow as tubers. In both cases the plants develop starchy food stores for their own use.

Cross-section of a Single Grain of Wheat

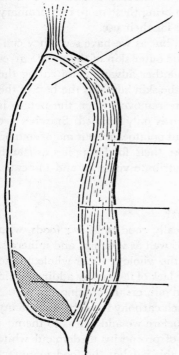

Endosperm: white part of grain used for white flour. White flour is then 'fortified' with B vitamins and iron to replace those removed by milling. White grains of starch are contained in cells with cellulose walls. Cell walls provide some fibre, but not a large amount.

Bran: the outer coat, not much food value but plenty of fibre. Bran and wheatgerm are removed in milling white flour.

Aleurone layer: just below the skin. Rich in protein and B vitamins, so another benefit for those who choose wholemeal bread.

Wheatgerm: contains protein and fat, together with iron and B vitamins. From this little store the root and shoot develop when a grain grows into a new plant.

Consider first a grain of wheat. It is a seed, a really beautiful object containing all the food needed to start a new plant growing. It is very small; the diagram (see p. 55) shows how it looks under a biologist's magnifying-glass. This picture of the wheat grain shows us that the carbohydrate comes from the endosperm part, where it is developed in close association with other nutrients. This picture would be true of many other grains—rye, barley, oats and rice. The shape of the grain would be different in each case but the various parts would be the same.

Our main supplies of starchy carbohydrates come from these foods and from potatoes. Nowadays spaghetti, macaroni and many other types of pasta are becoming very popular. These supply starchy carbohydrate, often from coarsely-milled white flour, but some are made from wholemeal flour and the makers of wholemeal pasta are seeking to bring these more into ordinary shops. Good recipes are available for their use.

Potatoes too are mainly starch, but as we have seen they contribute a little protein as well. The outer skin of the potato gives a good amount of extra fibre. Another advantage of eating the skin is that the thin layer under the skin contains the best of the vitamins and minerals, which are removed when the potato is peeled, but retained if the potato is only scraped. Starches are present in other root vegetables, but potatoes are our major source.

To sum up, where plants store their food supplies as starch we find valuable foods which contribute vitamins and minerals.

Which Starchy Foods are Best?

Whole grains and potatoes are really good satisfying foods, with a lot to offer in terms of flavour as well as vitamins and minerals. But as soon as we get away from the whole grain or whole potato we have to start compensating for lack of flavour by adding fats in the form of butter, frying fats and oils, cream or icing. These are the foods that help us eat too much carbohydrate, because many carbohydrate foods taste 'plain' before we add extras to them.

It has always been a symbol of prosperity to demand white flour, right through the ages, so this is what the food manufacturers have given us for our bread, cakes and pastries. As far as potatoes are concerned, a rhyme for children indicates the widespread attitude that the peel is not for eating:

> Dearly beloved brethren
> Is it not a sin
> When you peel a potato
> To throw away the skin?
> The skin feeds the pig
> And the pig feeds you
> Dearly beloved brethren
> Is not this true?

Potato peelings and the highly nutritious skins of other foods were always given to the pigs, but during the recent winter of poor potato harvest, which caused very high potato prices, many people began to eat the peel with great enjoyment. Our speciality is roasting small unpeeled potatoes around a joint of meat.

Starchy foods, as unpeeled and unprocessed as possible, are very unlikely to be the mainstays of overeating sprees. They are delicious, nutritious and very satisfying.

SUGARS

These are the sugar-containing carbohydrate foods you might bring home from shopping:

Fruits, containing fruit sugars known chemically as fructose. It is good to use these as the sweet things in our meals.

Dried fruits: prunes, figs, apricots and raisins. These are even sweeter than fresh fruit because the drying process has reduced their size. Chop dried fruits to add to muesli or breakfast cereals. Use to fill sandwiches for children. In these ways they are used in small quantities.

'Gran', 'Castor' and 'Icing', well-known members of the sugar family, are such comforting foods to have around! They are associated with hot, sweet drinks, silver sugar sifters and birthday cakes. Could this not perhaps be the enemy in disguise?

Honey and jam: however natural the honey bees and however full of fruit the jam, these are all highly concentrated carbohydrates. We may eat too much of them without realizing it.

Cakes and biscuits are usually made with white flour. They can be upgraded by using brown flour, much less sugar and sometimes vegetable oils.

FIBRE OR CELLULOSE

This comes from the fibrous parts of vegetables and fruits. The largest amounts of fibre are in the parts we frequently peel away. In cereals, such as oats, wheat, rye, barley and rice, a great deal of the fibre is concentrated in the bran, the outermost layer. Thus wholemeal bread contains three times as much fibre as white bread, and other brown breads contain about twice as much as white bread. Fibre is not broken down much during digestion but it is extremely useful in increasing the bulk and texture of our food and for this reason it is considered very important for health.

When we make up a shopping list, carbohydrate foods are very important items. Will the meal be based on bread, potatoes, pasta or rice as the main carbohydrate food, or shall we cut out starches and save our calories for a dessert based on white flour and sugar? Do we choose refined white flour, grain and sugar products or do we insist on whole foods? Does it ultimately make any difference which carbohydrates we choose as long as we don't overeat?

The Importance of Fibre in the Diet

If you have not yet read one of the recently published books about fibre in food, a summary of the discoveries being made about the importance of fibre may be helpful.

Interest in fibre arose when doctors working in rural Africa, where food is simple, unrefined and unprocessed, found that whereas many people died because of infections, there were far fewer illnesses and deaths due to heart disease, cancer, diabetes and strokes than in Western society—though when Africans moved to urban areas and a refined diet they also began to suffer from these ills. People in wealthier countries also suffer from obesity, diverticular disease, digestive problems, haemorrhoids, varicose veins, deep-vein thrombosis, hiatus hernias and gallstones, although these seldom occur in more primitive communities.

The suggested explanation is this: manufacturing processes often remove a considerable amount of fibre from food, particularly in the case of milling to make white flour and polished rice. This also happens when we meticulously peel fruit and vegetables. This means a change in the demands that food makes on the digestive tract. Food processing and preparing may actually usurp the function of the digestive tract. First, fibre needs chewing, so the teeth and jaws are well used, working hard as they were made to work. During the longer chewing process plenty of saliva (containing the first of the digestive enzymes) is mixed in with the food. This is the first stage of digestion and takes time if you are eating a wholemeal roll, but is often almost completely missed out as people eat a light slice of sponge cake or meringue, either of which 'melt in the mouth'. Fibre is also a good 'space-filler' when food enters the stomach. It is in itself bulky and causes more gastric juice to be secreted than more compact fibre-free food. The increased volume makes the meal more satisfying. Wholegrain food has 9 per cent fewer calories than refined white grain products, taken weight for weight, so tends to be less 'fattening'.

Fibre surrounding or accompanying carbohydrate (depending on whether you eat wholegrain or crushed grain foods) makes digestion a slower process. The speed at which carbohydrate enters the body by the bloodstream is therefore slower and more gradual. This is a good thing because it means that carbohydrate is less quickly turned into fat and less easily laid down as 'fattening' fat. Also the liver is less likely to pour cholesterol and triglycerides into the bloodstream after this kind of meal (see p. 73). This makes for healthier arteries.

It is interesting to know that from our 'modern' diets, 93 per cent of the total possible energy is released from our food, to be used as energy, or stored as fat if we have eaten above our requirements. On a fibre-rich diet only 88–89 per cent of the energy available is released, so you are immediately saving yourself from the over-effects of 4 or 5 per cent of your calories. People eating whole foods and little sugar tend to reach and keep to their ideal weight and avoid the tendency to overweight. A fibre-rich meal using wholemeal bread or unpolished rice, wholemeal pasta or beans, which are digested and absorbed more slowly, also tends to be a bulky meal, which allows the satiety mechanisms to operate normally so that normal weight can be preserved throughout life. No wild animal is ever overweight; there must be a lesson here in connection with eating more unprocessed foods.

Does Fibre Prevent Illnesses?

We have seen how the presence of fibre makes chewing, digesting and absorbing food more effective and 'right' for the body. What then of the claims that an adequate amount of fibre in our food prevents such things as a tendency to diverticular disease, digestive problems, haemorrhoids, varicose veins, deep-vein thrombosis and hiatus hernia? The suggestion is that foods with the fibre removed form waste products that pass more slowly through the bowel. Some waste products remain in the bowel for a considerable time, longer in some people than in others. Pressure builds up, constipation results, and sometimes there are 'blow outs' of the walls of the bowel into small balloon-like diverticuli. This is diverticulitis. A healthy bowel has soft but flexible muscular walls and is best kept healthy by soft and bulky food containing fibre, which will form high-volume, bulky waste products, rapidly moving through the bowel and easily passed out of the body. There is the added advantage that if there should be carcinogenic (cancer-causing) elements in the food they are moved out of the body quickly, rather than being kept around for a longer time and possibly absorbed into the bloodstream.

High pressures in the bowel, due to a predominance of refined foods, can cause distension, nausea, heartburn, belching, headaches, weakness and fainting. Haemorrhoids and varicose veins are thought to be caused by pressure in the bowel region constricting the great veins as they work to return blood to the heart from the legs and lower parts of the abdomen. Symptoms of diverticular disease, and the so-called 'Irritable Bowel Syndrome', can be removed by adding bran to the diet, but the suggestion is that many of these unpleasant complaints may actually be prevented by choosing a diet containing a reasonable amount of fibre. It is interesting to follow the train of thought behind the varicose veins theory: African women have many children and don't get varicose veins. They stand or stoop in the fields all day and don't get varicose veins. The difference is in their diet: their food is often twice as rich in fibre as ours is.

All the illnesses mentioned are of the kind which can develop in a 'hidden' way and then suddenly appear in more extreme forms in middle or old age. At an early stage the condition may not have been troublesome, but the more advanced stage may be very serious indeed. It has been said that 60 per cent of sixty-year-olds have some diverticular disease.

There are also indications that people eating full-fibre diets are less susceptible to diabetes and gallstones. Space does not permit an explanation of these suggestions but it is well worth reading about them in one of the books dealing specifically with the importance of fibre.

The Link Between Fibre and Heart Disease

For a number of years there has been a hypothesis that there might well be such a link, based on the observed lack of coronary heart disease amongst races where the fibre content of the diet is high. Now, in a British survey on men, carried out over a period of twenty years, it has been shown that *men with a high energy intake had a lower rate of coronary heart disease than the rest, and, independently of this, so did men with a high intake of dietary fibre from cereals.*

The high-energy intake indicates that the men were fairly active. Lack of exercise has for a long time been thought to be one of the important factors in heart disease. And the protective value of having a high intake of dietary fibre from cereals is one of the most important nutritional discoveries of this century.

Fibre Helps to Fight Dental Caries

Dental caries and gum diseases are largely problems of present-day Western civilizations. In fact, dental caries is the commonest disease in these countries, and it is a disease brought about by eating the wrong food. Rural populations in primitive countries suffer from it far less than we do.

Cavities are caused in the following way. Saliva causes a microscopic layer of protein called pellicle to form on the surface of each tooth. If you eat sugar and refined starch products, the pellicle layer will become impregnated with organisms present in saliva and carbohydrate debris. The layer is then known as plaque. (This can be detected on the teeth as a furry feeling if one is unable to brush one's teeth during the day.) If you continue to supply plenty of sugar the bacteria in the plaque will be well fed. They will then produce acids which make holes in the teeth.

The importance of daily teeth-cleaning is that plaque must be removed from the teeth on a regular basis, to prevent caries and gum diseases. If wholegrain foods are eaten in preference to refined products, the build-up of plaque does not occur. (A Swiss doctor removed the problem of dental caries almost completely for one group of children by persuading the local baker to make wholemeal bread and the parents to forbid sweet-eating.)

HOW MUCH FIBRE DO WE NEED?

Individual requirements for fibre have not yet been worked out. What we do know is that whereas rural Africans eat about 25 g fibre each day, people in Western society have been assessed as averaging 6·4 g per day. This means of course that some of us take much less than 6·4 g. The sort of fibre intakes that help people with constipation and diverticular disease are of the order of 10–15 g per day.

The low fibre intakes arise where people make a virtue of never eating bread, porridge or breakfast cereals, thus removing cereal fibre from their meals. Their argument would be that they get plenty of roughage from fruit and vegetables, but two points which counter this argument should be borne in mind:

1. Cereal fibre intake has been shown to be a factor in preventing coronary heart disease (see p. 61). So we cannot ignore its importance.
2. In order to get 10 g fibre from fruit and vegetables alone we should need to eat about 2½ lb (over 1 kg) of those fruits and vegetables which have a high fibre content. An example would be 3½ oz (100 g) each of peas, carrots, cabbage, green beans, broccoli, Brussels sprouts, potato twice, tomatoes twice, plus a large apple and a banana all in one day! And you would still miss out the specific value of having cereal fibre.

How to Increase Fibre Intake
It is easier to do this effectively with cereal foods, although eating more fruit and vegetables will help significantly too. Here are some practical suggestions:

—Change to wholemeal bread.
—Choose other carbohydrate foods which contain fibre (see p. 65).
—Try homemade muesli for breakfast. Here is a recipe for a good mixture to make up in bulk in a polythene box:
  8 oz (225 g) rolled oats, 3 oz (90 g) wheatgerm, 2 oz (60 g) bran, 4 oz (115 g) chopped hazel nuts, 4 oz (115 g) raisins, 2 oz (60 g) chopped dried apricots. A 2 oz (60 g) portion of this muesli gives 6 g fibre and also provides 6·6 g mixed protein; taken with 4 fl oz (120 ml) milk this would total 11 g protein; it therefore makes a valuable breakfast food.
—Eat porridge sometimes.
—A large salad of shredded raw vegetables, such as cabbage, carrots, celery and peppers, makes a good vegetable fibre addition as well as providing extra vitamins and minerals. Some people make this a daily addition to lunch.

64   The Case for Carbohydrates

If your meals look like this you are likely to be taking enough fibre

If your meals look like this it would be a good idea to think about upgrading your fibre intake

Morning
Fruit juice
Muesli, porridge or
   wholegrain cereal
Egg
Brown bread or toast

Morning
Fruit juice
Refined breakfast cereal
Egg
White bread or toast

Midday
Cheese salad using
   shredded raw vegetables
Brown roll and butter

Midday
Ploughman's lunch with
French bread

Evening
Meat casserole with carrots
Potatoes, green vegetable
Fruit pudding with brown flour
   pastry or crumble

Evening
Meat casserole served with
   white rice and peas
Icecream with fudge sauce

Can We Keep to Refined Foods and Just Add Bran to Compensate?

When we eat refined foods we are providing the body with carbohydrate in a concentrated, easy-to-absorb state, and many people believe that the human body is not designed to handle food in this form. If we eat bran to counteract the effects of having little cereal fibre in our white bread, cakes, biscuits and breakfast cereals, certainly that should help to prevent the illnesses which relate to the large bowel and some of the associated conditions (varicose veins, haemorrhoids, hiatus hernias, leg thrombosis).

What we do not achieve with bran is to replace the unique quality of wholegrain food, in which carbohydrate is 'diluted' by the presence of bran, digested more slowly, and so released into the bloodstream more slowly. It is this effect, together with the calorie-saving effect (see p. 60), that is desirable in the prevention of diabetes, overweight and possibly also gallstones.

Bran is good for us but wholegrain foods are better.

A GUIDE TO SELECTING THE BEST OF CARBOHYDRATE FOODS

Carbohydrate foods are good for us, provided that we choose wisely.

Choose Carbohydrate Foods that Include Fibre

If we want to include more fibre-rich foods in our meals, we should choose:

> Wholemeal bread
> Wholemeal flour
> Whole brown rice
> Wholemeal macaroni, spaghetti, lasagne, also 'green pasta' (made with spinach)
> Oatmeal
> Digestive biscuits
> Wholewheat crispbreads
> Wholewheat cereals (e.g. shredded and wholewheat biscuit types)
> Muesli (homemade if possible)
> Potatoes
> All vegetables (including frozen or canned ones)
> Fruits (including dried fruits)
> Nuts
> Dried peas, beans and lentils (including ready-cooked ones which have been frozen or canned)
> Jams (better homemade, and choose those which include the skins such as coarse-cut marmalade and blackcurrant jam)

The foods which will inevitably be replaced are white bread

and buns, white rice and pasta, sugary breakfast cereals, cream biscuits, jelly jams, white flour and sugar-based cakes and puddings, canned fruits in heavy syrup. Other foods containing white flour are instant puddings, packet sauces and soups, cake mixes, canned meats and baby foods.

Choose Carbohydrate Foods that Contain Protein

Referring back to the chapter on protein, it will be remembered that of the foods listed above nuts, dried peas, beans and lentils are good sources of protein. Wholewheat and whole rice products and oatmeal also provide useful amounts of protein because of the relatively substantial quantities in which they are eaten. This is why choosing these multi-purpose foods is more sensible than overloading the diet with sugary foods which contain carbohydrate only.

Choose Carbohydrate Foods that Contain Vitamin B_1

This vitamin will be considered later in the book, but it has to be mentioned here because it is the vitamin which sparks off the chain of reactions by which carbohydrate foods are converted into energy. Carbohydrate without vitamin B_1 will never give energy; it is chemically impossible. Looking back to the list, it is the flour and cereal products, peas, beans, lentils and nuts which have good supplies of this vitamin. Sugar does not have it, so if we choose sugar for carbohydrate then the vitamin B_1 must be supplied by other foods.

Getting Along Without Sugar

It makes good sense to cut sugar out of our meals as much as possible. The fruits we eat will give us some sugar, in the form of fructose. This is good and the quantity is not great anyway. If we begin to eat less sugar we gradually want less. The amount can easily be cut down in biscuit, cake, custard and pudding recipes. Fruit can be stewed with very little sugar, and breakfast cereals taste very good without it—you really find out what oats and wheat taste like. Remember that soft and fizzy drinks all contain sugar. They are bad for children's teeth and contain 'hidden calories' because they go down so fast! Bread is very good just spread with butter or peanut butter. Conserves of minced fruits, cooked for a short time with very little sugar, and possibly added pectin, then frozen till required, make low-sugar spreads. Apple purée is good too—and these fruit 'spreads' also give vitamin C. Many people are addicted to sugar. It is good to bring children up to prefer savoury things and to rely on dried fruits and nuts for treats.

Which Carbohydrate Foods Cause People to Overeat?
—White bread thickly buttered.
—Potato chips or crisps with their appetizing crisp fried surface.
—Pastries, particularly those made from puff or choux paste, often with rich fillings as well.
—Light sponge cakes filled with cream or topped with icing.
—Chocolate biscuits and cream filled biscuits (which are the manufacturers' best-selling lines).

A Store Cupboard of Well-chosen Carbohydrate Foods is the Best Aid to Better Choice
This will always contain wholemeal flour, bread and crispbreads, homemade cookies (using brown flour, oatmeal, nuts), brown rice, brown pasta, porridge oats, muesli, brown breakfast cereals, dried fruit (apricots, figs, prunes, sultanas, raisins). Potatoes, root vegetables and fruit will also provide the right carbohydrates.

6. Fats and Oils are Controversial

Fats and oils are controversial because many people have become concerned about a link between the amount and type of fat in our everyday food and the heart and artery diseases which have become major illnesses in the Western world.

Lack of sufficient cereal fibre in our meals has now been cited as an important contributory factor. Lack of exercise, smoking and anxiety are other aspects to be aware of. Shortages of vitamin B_6 and chromium also appear to be linked with the problem (see pp. 110–11 and 78–80). No one is completely sure which factors matter most but the picture is becoming clearer each year. One thing is certain: in Britain and the USA people are eating on average twice as much fat as they really need. And much of that fat is of the kind which contributes to high blood-cholesterol levels and silted-up arteries. Apart from anything else, too much fat gives too many calories and causes overweight. In order to describe the known facts about fats and oils it may be helpful to consider a few basic questions.

HOW MANY FOODS CONTAIN FAT?

Your list probably includes butter, margarine, lard, cooking fats and oils, cream, icecream, the fat on meat, milk and cheese. Now consider the 'hidden fat' that is present in the lean part of meat and bacon, the fat in puddings, cakes, pastries and sauces, the oils in nuts and in the oily fish such as herring, mackerel, salmon, tuna and sardines. Hidden fats usually add up to 50 per cent of our total fat intake.

The following chart shows which foods contain the most fat.

PERCENTAGE OF CALORIES FROM FAT IN FOODS
(Remember in looking at this chart that fat gives twice as many calories weight for weight as protein or carbohydrate.)

Over 50 per cent calories from fat

Roast pork
Pork chops
Roast lamb
Sausages
Cooked ham
Fried liver
Steak and kidney pie
Herrings

Sardines
Eggs
Most cheeses, cheese spreads
Peanuts, peanut butter, other
  nuts
Icecream
Victoria sandwich cake

Over 40 per cent calories from fat

Stewed steak
Best roasts of beef
Salmon, canned
Milk

Rice pudding
Bread and butter pudding
Apple pie

Over 30 per cent calories from fat

Roast chicken or turkey
Sirloin, flank or shin of beef

Rich fruit cake
Trifle

Over 20 per cent calories from fat

Pot-roasted beef
Grilled liver

White meat only of roast
  chicken
Fish fingers, grilled

Under 20 per cent calories from fat

White fish: haddock, cod,
  halibut, plaice, sole*
Bread, porridge, breakfast
  cereals

Peas, beans, lentils
Skimmed milk, yoghurt
Low fat cheeses, especially
  cottage cheese

* Percentage given for white fish refers to uncooked fish, as choice of cooking method may greatly influence fat content.

IS FAT ESSENTIAL FOR HEALTH?

Could we not make good meals from just protein and carbo-hydrate? It would be difficult for the following reasons:

Fat is Important for Flavour

It is hard to make meals taste good without any fat at all. In any case many foods contain fat as part of their structure. Additional fat is needed to make many foods enjoyable: the butter on bread, the oil brushed on meat or fish before grilling, the French dressing on a salad. These are modest examples of adding fat or oil to food. The percentage of fat in meals begins to soar when people eat fried foods often and regularly take cream on desserts.

Some Vitamins are Fat-soluble

Some of the important vitamins come to us 'dissolved' in the fats and oils we eat. These vitamins, A, D, E and K, are known as the fat-soluble vitamins. They do not dissolve in water as all the other vitamins do, so if we cut out fats and oils we would be short of them.

Certain 'Essential Fatty Acids' are Needed for Growth

These are some of the complex chemicals of which fats and oils are composed and in certain animals they have been shown to be needed for growth. Obviously no one is going to experiment with human infants, but it is reasonable to assume that children need them too, so we should make sure they are adequately re-presented in the diet.

Fat is a Useful Energy Food

For youngsters and people doing heavy work and needing lots of calories, fats and oils are concentrated foods in terms of energy giving power. Less energetic people need to make sure they eat less fat.

Our Protective Fat Store Must Be Maintained

Fat present under the skin protects our bodies from injury. In certain areas of the body there is internal fat which protects organs such as the kidneys.

BASIC TYPES OF FATS AND OILS

All fats and oils are mixtures of fatty acids (just as proteins are mixtures of amino acids). The mixture can vary in ingredients and quantities, so there are a lot of factors to consider in assessing the nature of a particular fat or oil. Most people will have heard of saturated fats and poly-unsaturated fats. There are also mono-unsaturated fats, but for simplicity we are going to concentrate only on the other two kinds.

The saturated fats and oils are the ones we are advised to eat less of, replacing them where possible with poly-unsaturated fats and oils.

Foods containing mainly saturated fats and oils

Beef, pork and mutton fat
Butter, margarine and lard
Cooking fats
Coconut oil
Milk
Cheese

Foods containing mainly poly-unsaturated fats and oils

Maize oil, i.e. corn oil
Sunflower or sunflower seed oil
Safflower oil
Soya bean oil
Most nuts (except cashews and coconuts)
Fish
Fish oils (including the oils in herrings, mackerel, kippers, pilchards, sardines, tuna, salmon)
Fish liver oils (cod and halibut)

Foods containing a balance of poly-unsaturated and saturated fats and oils
The special margarines, labelled 'high in poly-unsaturated fats'
   and generally stating percentages
The special 'low saturated fat cheese', developed in Australia
Palm oil

THE IMPORTANCE OF CHOOSING FATS AND OILS CAREFULLY

Hardening of the arteries (atherosclerosis) is a disease in which
the arteries that were originally healthy (picture 1) come to look
in cross-section like picture 2. The space in the centre of these
blood vessels, through which our blood is meant to flow, gets less
and less.

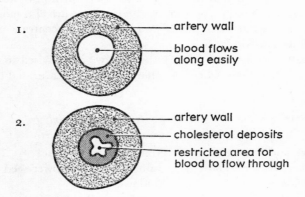

We know that this silting-up process can start in childhood and
continue into adolescence and adulthood, getting worse as people
grow older. However, it has been shown that children who have
been brought up to drink skimmed milk (i.e. milk from which the
fat has been removed) have healthier arteries than those who have
always had whole milk. (It is important to note, however, that
skimmed milk is not to be used for feeding infants; for them the
choice is either mother's milk or a carefully chosen substitute.)

The problem is even more significant for adults. If we treat ourselves to the richest milk, eat plenty of cream and add a knob of butter to every dish, we may be helping ourselves to artery disease. Our choice of meat and our cooking methods also merit some scrutiny.

High intakes of fat appear to contribute to heart and artery trouble, but reducing the total fat intake is just part of the dietary change suggested. The next part is to change the type of fat to some extent. Convincing experiments have shown that the death rate from coronary disease was almost halved in two groups of men who were each for six years given food containing special 'poly-unsaturated' margarine and 'filled' milk (milk in which the saturated fat has been replaced by unsaturated fat).

There are two main conditions which if arising may contribute to heart disease:

1. Hypertension, or high blood pressure.
2. Atherosclerosis, or hardening of the arteries.

Both hypertension and atherosclerosis are often associated with overweight, owing to eating too much and exercising too little. It has been suggested that the best way to prepare for a healthy retirement is to get one's weight down, if necessary, to the average weight recommended for one's height. The occurrence of atherosclerosis is also linked with the level of cholesterol and triglycerides in the blood.

WHAT IS CHOLESTEROL?

Cholesterols are fatty substances found in quite small quantities in animal fats. They are also manufactured in the human body. The amount we make is influenced by our weight, the amount of exercise we take and the amount and type of fat we eat. High blood-cholesterol levels mean that a lot of blood cholesterol is being carried around the body in the bloodstream.

For many years it had been thought that if the total blood-cholesterol level is high it is bad for the arteries. Recently it has been shown that the picture is not so simple. Interesting information has come from research carried out over a period of twenty-six years in a town in Massachusetts, where half the adults between the ages of thirty and sixty were studied. Five groups of substances containing cholesterol are known to occur in the bloodstream and, of these, two have been identified as being particularly important: alpha cholesterol and beta cholesterol.

Alpha cholesterol seems to act in removing cholesterol from the body, and the more alpha cholesterol people have, the less risk there is of coronary heart disease. High levels of beta cholesterol, on the other hand, increase this risk. The level of beta cholesterol is related to our intake of foods containing cholesterol and saturated fats.

How can we increase our alpha cholesterol levels and thereby get all the protection possible? Two groups of people have been shown to have higher than average levels of alpha cholesterol:

1. Those taking regular strenuous exercise.
2. Those eating vegetarian food, or vegetarian food plus fish.

This does not necessarily mean that we should stop eating meat, but it does suggest we should eat vegetable protein foods and fish in place of some of our meat. There are other ways, too, in which the well-informed food-chooser can cut down a family's total intake of fat, saturated fat in particular, and also of cholesterol.

HOW TO EAT LESS FAT OVERALL, USING POLY-UNSATURATED FATS AND OILS WHEREVER POSSIBLE

—Choose lean meats where possible.
—Remember that sausages and some canned meats are likely to have a high fat content.
—Eat fish or chicken in place of some meat meals.
—Buy skimmed milk (fresh or reconstituted from skimmed milk powder) for adults or older children. Small children need whole milk.

—Increase the amount of cereals you eat, including bread, porridge, rice and pasta, at the same time increasing vegetable and nut intake. Vegetarian meals to replace some of our meat meals are helpful in this respect.

—Use a special margarine (high in poly-unsaturated fats) for spreading.

—Pot-roast or casserole meat, then skim the fat off before serving.

—Grill wherever possible. For frying use a non-stick pan and a light brushing of oil.

—Look carefully at recipes and work out how much fat there is per person, then make a black list. Make a white list, too, of recipes which do not have too much fat, otherwise you may run short of ideas after banishing some old favourites.

—Cakes and pastry can be made with corn oil or special margarine (high in poly-unsaturated fats) instead of butter.

—Scrambled eggs can be made with a spoonful of corn oil or special margarine, instead of butter; oil can also be added to vegetables before serving.

—Sauces can be made with a roux of oil or special margarine instead of butter or margarine. The mixture is 1 tablespoon oil to 2 level tablespoons flour to ½ pint (300 ml) liquid.

Even when you are cutting down on saturated fats there is still plenty of scope for good cooking. The best recipes are likely to come from the wholefood cookbooks, and the extra ingredients more from the greengrocer than from the dairy section of the shops. Risottos, bean soups and pasta dishes can all be made without any saturated fat at all.

Some traditional sauces are very high in saturated fat content and include egg yolks too, which are particularly high in cholesterol. For example, Bearnaise sauce for six people has 8 oz (225 g) butter and three egg yolks, while Hollandaise sauce has 8 oz (225 g) butter and two egg yolks.

On the following page there are some suggestions for sauces with a low fat content. Skimmed milk and oil or special margarine can be used instead of whole milk and butter in those recipes marked with an asterisk.

Tomato and onion sauce
Tomato and green pepper sauce
Vegetable sauce
Barbecue sauce
Gooseberry sauce
Plum sauce

Apple sauce
Cranberry sauce
Curry sauce
Parsley sauce*
Onion sauce*

HOW TO EAT LESS FOODS CONTAINING CHOLESTEROL

Below is a list of foods containing cholesterol expressed as mg per 100 g (3½ oz). The US Dietary Goals suggest that we should reduce our cholesterol consumption to about 300 mg a day (see p. 29). However, it has not been proved that it is necessary for everyone to adopt such radical changes of diet. Also the figures below show only total cholesterol and do not distinguish between α and β types.

Egg yolk	1,500	Fish roe	300 plus
Whole egg	550	Oysters	200 plus
Egg white	0	Lobster	200
Butter	250	Crab	125
Cheese	100	Shrimps	125
Milk	11	Fish	70
Brains	2,000 plus	Lard	95
Kidney	375	Margarine (part animal fat)	65
Liver	300		
Sweetbreads	250	Margarine (all vegetable fat)	0
Heart	150		
Veal	90	Vegetable oils	0
Pork	70	Cereals	0
Beef	70	Fruit	0
Mutton	65	Vegetables	0
Chicken	60		

When looking at charts like these one has to bear in mind what quantity of each particular food makes a reasonable serving. For example 100 g egg yolk amounts to about six yolks, and you are likely to eat only one or two at a time, whereas you might easily eat the 100 g portion of roast beef. You will need to use a calculator to explore this in detail. However, the meat and fish portions eaten are likely to be of similar size.

To Eat Less Cholesterol

—Eat more vegetables, fruits, pulses and cereals.

—Eat correspondingly less meat.

—Meats to choose are chicken, lean lamb, mutton, beef or veal, though liver and kidney should be included occasionally because the iron value is so good and because of another vitamin B_{12}.

—Brains, sweetbreads and heart are not so popular anyway, but if you do like them let the rule be to have them only very occasionally and in small quantities. A dish described as Escalope de Ris de Veau is a nutritionist's nightmare: sweetbreads are first braised, then coated in egg and breadcrumbs, shallow-fried and served with nut-brown butter.

—Fish is a good alternative to meat, because although the total cholesterol value may be similar fish does not contain saturated fats.

—Eggs are a problem because they are so ever-ready and so versatile. They are useful for protein and for iron, yet for adults many nutritionists recommend limiting eggs to only three a week. This has to include the eggs used for cooking. My own family food planning is not as extreme as this. I tend to buy $1\frac{1}{2}$ or 2 dozen eggs a week for a family of four—never large, always standard or medium—which means four to six a week each. We have homemade cakes and biscuits, so some of the eggs used are shared with visitors. I am inclined to think that spreading a modest number of eggs throughout the diet may one day be proved to be the most important thing. Perhaps more harmful effects occur if we eat a three-egg omelette now and again and suddenly overload our system with cholesterol. In the light of recent findings I also expect my family to gain some protection against heart disease from the amount of cereal fibre we always eat.

—Shrimps and crab are a better choice than lobster and oysters, but only the very wealthy, or expense account diners, are going to be seriously troubled by such problems.

Many people argue that we do not yet have the full medical picture on the subject of saturated fats and cholesterol, but while research continues I think we can at least benefit by making use of the knowledge we already have.

The Value of Chromium

Before leaving this topic I think it is wise to highlight one mineral from the trace elements described in the chapter on vitamins and minerals. This mineral is chromium, and it may also be important in the prevention of atherosclerosis.

Until recently chromium has been regarded as an element which, although necessary, need not be the subject of special attention in the matter of food choice. It is not usual to find much about chromium in nutrition textbooks, and if you do look it up you are likely to find that chromium is thought to be necessary for maintaining the correct level of glucose in the blood. Also that people suffering from diabetes seem to need more of this element and that low blood-sugar problems in some elderly people may be due to chromium deficiency. This would be sufficient to make most people close the book and concentrate on some more significant aspect of nutrition. In fact a lot of interesting research has been done on chromium, and these are some of the facts:

a. Newborn babies have good stores of chromium in their bodies.
b. Children brought up on unrefined foods keep these stores high. If they then continue to eat unrefined foods during adult life they do not develop low chromium levels.
c. Those who eat white flour products, refined breakfast cereals and refined sugars suffer a lowering of chromium levels which continues throughout life, so that by the age of fifty some

people have no chromium left and others very little. The problem about trying to put this right is that chromium is very difficult to absorb, except in regular minute amounts throughout life, and one cannot just take pills to redress the balance.

This matters because there seems to be a close correlation between the chromium level in our bodies and atherosclerosis.

Atherosclerosis is responsible for heart attacks and for strokes. For years scientists have been looking for the ideal diet to prevent people having heart attacks. What is needed is something to prevent fatty deposits building up in the arteries.

In countries where unrefined foods are eaten, where most of the calories come from unrefined grains, and sugar is taken from raw sugar cane or honey, there is little heart disease. But if people in such countries are introduced to a Western type of diet (with refined foods), after about twenty years it begins to appear. Twenty years is the time taken for the youngsters to reach middle age, having eaten refined foods for much of their lives.

What the refined-food eaters are missing is fibre, and with it some micro-nutrients. One of these is chromium. It is possible to demonstrate what happens by feeding animals on a refined food, Western-style diet. If a very small amount of chromium is always added to their food the animals' cholesterol levels remain low. If no chromium is given they develop serious atherosclerosis. The point of demonstrating this in animals is that they reach maturity very quickly and the research scientist does not have to wait for years to find out what happens to them in middle age.

How to Maintain Our Chromium Levels

Foods good for chromium are wholewheat products, oatmeal, brown rice, raw sugars (meaning the very dark brown sugar in which you can taste the molasses), honey, maple syrup and unsweetened fruit juices. Of the foods of animal origin, chicken and shellfish contain the most chromium. By eating wisely we can retain our chromium stores at their present level. It is not very clear to what extent we can put things right if we are older and our stores are very low, but there is still the option of changing to meals containing less saturated fat and cholesterol in order to protect our health.

One of the most important things is to make sure that our children grow up liking unrefined foods so that habits are formed and they are likely to continue to prefer 'brown' to 'white'. They will then never suffer from chromium depletion and will stand a better chance of enjoying good health in the later years of their lives. After all, in suggesting foods to eat for chromium we are not suggesting anything odd or unusual. We are simply saying that the same best choices for carbohydrate foods and for fibre in our meals happen to keep us well supplied with chromium too. This also ties in well with the idea of using some vegetarian foods to reduce the fat and cholesterol in our meals and brings us back to our original chapter theme.

7. Freedom from Calorie-counting

Calories have become famous because of the emphasis on slimming which has predominated over all other nutritional information produced for general consumption in recent years. Now ideas about slimming are being revolutionized as research has shown the importance of eating full-fibre foods to counteract obesity. We might say that 'calories are out' and 'fibre is in'. By removing the fibre from our food we remove nature's brake on overeating. Unrefined foods, as has been shown in the carbohydrate chapter, can easily be eaten in over-large quantities. The same is not true of wholegrain products, which give a lasting feeling of fullness as well as providing energy. It is basically the type of food we eat that causes obesity, not just the quantity.

The interest in a link between eating full-fibre foods and keeping slim arose when it was noted that in rural Africa obesity is very rare indeed, while Africans who had lived for a time on a Western type of diet, with a predominance of refined carbohydrate, soon became overweight. The feeling of fullness given by refined foods does not last nearly as long as that given by a full-fibre meal. This is because with wholegrain foods the bulk of the meal is greater in relation to the number of calories, and also because the carbohydrate is released more slowly over a longer period of time so that people do not become hungry for between-meals snacks. Their energy level stays high for longer and there is less likelihood of carbohydrate being converted into stored fat.

Overweight people often feel very 'empty', and this is literally true if their food is low in fibre and not very filling. Many people who change to full-fibre meals, starting to eat wholemeal bread, jacket potatoes and brown rice, find that they quite easily lose weight and then stabilize at a sensible weight for their height. It is interesting that vegetarians are 10 per cent slimmer on average than omnivores. This is partly due to the fibrous nature of their food. People who eat whole foods do not have to worry so much about calories, provided they are not addicted to sugar. Sugar-eaters live dangerously because sugar-eating is the best (or worst) way of taking in too much food without being aware of what you are doing. Nature intended us to eat sugar with its fibre, as in sugar cane or fruits. Their chewiness and bulk prevent overeating.

The guidelines for losing weight are the same as for optimum health and fitness:

—Increase your consumption of wholegrain foods, fruit and vegetables.
—Cut out sugar and foods with a high sugar content.
—Decrease the amount of fat you eat.
—Decrease the amount of meat you eat and substitute meals of fish, chicken, beans or lentils.
—Decrease your consumption of salt and salty foods.
—Make sure you drink enough water. You need more when eating full-fibre foods.

Following these guidelines is easier than counting calories, and the bonus is that this way of eating contributes to general good health as well as helping with weight problems. However, we are not always fortunate enough to be eating in circumstances where well-informed people have chosen the menu, so it is worth knowing a little about calorie values so that we can avoid the obvious pitfalls. Also the world does seem to be somewhat unfairly divided into 'hard-gainers' who can eat a lot without putting on weight and 'easy-gainers' who quickly run to fat. The subject of calories is of more interest to the second group.

Those who have a lot of weight to lose will certainly do so more quickly if they choose lower-calorie-value foods for their full-fibre meals. This chapter is concerned with getting to know which foods have high calorie values and which have low ones, also with learning to spot the 'hidden calories' which make a food more fattening than it might appear to be.

For most people, however, an obsession with calorie-counting on a year-in, year-out basis is not a good thing. A continuous cycle of gaining weight and then losing it again is not good for us. It is better to stabilize your weight at a level that is right for your height, eating satisfying meals, and then forget about it.

KILOCALORIES AND KILOJOULES (KCAL AND KJ)

These are the units by which body energy is measured. Whatever amount of energy you use in a day, that day's food should be designed to provide an equal amount. Kilocalories are the old units of measurement, kilojoules the new metric ones. If the food we eat provides more energy than we need we store the extra energy as fat, like a fuel store, and there is weight gain. If the food provides less energy than we need the body draws on its reserves of fat and there is weight loss. One thing is certain though: it is much easier to gain weight than it is to lose it!

Below is an estimate of how much energy people need each day. Individual requirements vary; these are average figures.

	kcal	*kJ*
Adult man	2,700–3,500	11,300–15,000
Adult woman	2,200–2,500	9,200–10,500
Teenage boys	2,800–3,000	11,700–12,600
Teenage girls	2,300	9,600
Children		
(depending on age)	1,200–2,500	5,000–10,500
Infants up to 1 year	800	3,300

A Note on Terminology for Anyone Who Feels Confused
We talk about calorie requirements but we express them in kilocalories (each kilocalorie = 1,000 small calories). Magazine articles sometimes talk about 100 calorie portions, where they should write 100 kilocalories or kcal. This has also been expressed as 100 Calories, using a large C to denote kilocalories.

From now on kilojoules will gradually replace kilocalories in food tables. 1,000 kilojoules (kJ) is equivalent to 239 kilocalories (kcal).

To save everyone having to use calculators and losing the benefit of what they already know about 100 kcal portions, a convenient way of thinking about energy values has evolved: 95 kcal is equivalent to 400 kJ. As 95 kcal portions of food are nearly the same as 100 kcal portions, energy values can easily be expressed on these two bases.

HOW TO LIMIT YOUR CALORIE INTAKE

Calories come from protein and fat as well as from carbohydrate and so you have to make your choice from a wide range of foods, taking care not to exceed whatever is your own maximum requirement. Look at some of the 95 kcal (400 kJ) portions given below. Realize that if you require 2,000 kcal (8,400 kJ) you will only be able to have twenty-one such portions each day. For 2,500 kcal (10,500 kJ) one would choose twenty-six portions, and so on. If you are shopping and cooking for yourself it is easy to make sure that these portions are selected from foods which supply important nutrients as well as giving calories. Beware of the kind of pre-prepared foods which are very concentrated sources of calories with little else to offer nutritionally. Note that where the portions are very large, e.g. cauliflower, strawberries, you will only use a quarter or half portion from your allowance of portions.

95 kcal (400 kJ) Portions of Food Which are Largely Carbohydrate and in Some Cases Provide Vegetable Protein

Some of these portions are approximations.

Group 1

1 oz (30 g) rice, uncooked, 2 level tablespoons

1½ oz (45 g) wholemeal bread, 1 large slice

4 oz (115 g) potato, 1 medium sized
5 oz (140 g) baked beans
1¼ oz (38 g) lentils, uncooked, 2 level tablespoons
¾ oz (22 g) oats, made into porridge with water
1 oz breakfast cereal, average small portion
1 oz spaghetti, uncooked, small portion

Group 2
3 Marie biscuits
2 chocolate nut cookies
6 small cheese biscuits
2½ cream crackers
1 small chocolate biscuit snack
1 thick slice Swiss roll
½ individual jam tart
½ chocolate eclair, cream filled
1 small chocolate marshmallow
½ mince pie
½ large fruit scone
3 heaped teaspoons sugar
2 boiled sweets

95 kcal (400 kJ) Portions of Foods Which Provide Animal Protein

2 oz (60 g) chicken, roast, weighed without bone
1½ oz (45 g) beef, roast or casseroled
2 oz (60 g) liver, grilled
¾ oz (22 g) bacon, grilled
4½ oz (130 g) white fish, weighed before cooking
1½ oz (45 g) herring or mackerel, weighed before cooking
2 oz (60 g) fish fingers
2 oz (60 g) canned salmon, half a small can
1½ oz (45 g) canned sardines
¼ pint (150 ml) whole milk
¾ oz (22 g) cheese, Cheddar or similar
3 oz (90 g) cottage cheese

(see over)

    1 large egg
    1½ individual cartons plain yoghurt
    1 individual carton fruit yoghurt
    1 scoop of icecream, sufficient for a cone

95 kcal (400 kJ) Portions of Some Vegetables

    4 oz (115 g) boiled potato
    1½ oz (45 g) French fried potatoes
    5 oz (140 g) green peas
    1 lb (450 g) runner beans
    1 lb (450 g) carrots
    6 oz (170 g) parsnips
    1 whole small cauliflower
    1 whole small cabbage
    1 whole celery

95 kcal (400 kJ) Portions of Some Fruits

    7 oz (200 g) apples, 2 small
    9 oz (255 g) oranges, 2 small
    4 oz (115 g) banana, 1 small
    1 lb (450 g) grapefruit, 1 very large or 2 small
    1 lb (450 g) melon
    8 oz (225 g) peaches
    10 oz (280 g) plums
    12 oz (340 g) strawberries

95 kcal (400 kJ) Portions of Some High Fat Foods

    ½ oz (15 g) butter or margarine
    less than ½ oz (15 g) lard or cooking fat
    1 oz (30 g) low fat spread
    less than 1 oz (30 g) double cream
    2 oz (60 g) single cream

Calories from Foods Which Are Largely Carbohydrate

The energy values of some cereal foods, potatoes and pulses are shown, together with the values of some flour-based products. It is easy to see that the foods in Group 1 are more satisfying than those in Group 2 and that they contain more protein, fibre and vitamin B₁. More detail may be obtained by studying a book of food tables.

Calories from Foods Which Provide Animal Protein

Weight-watchers will choose lean meats and know that some meats are especially suitable: chicken, stewed steak, tripe (and liver and kidney occasionally, bearing in mind their high cholesterol content). White fish is even more useful with its low energy values. When considering meat and fish, it is important to remember that the way in which the food is cooked makes a great difference to its energy value. For example, frying adds fat and so adds calories really fast. Grilling, on the other hand, actually tends to reduce the energy value as the fat drips out. This is particularly so in the case of sausages and bacon. The following chart enables us to compare the calorie values of 3 oz (90 g) portions of a number of meats and fish, because 3 oz (90 g) is a reasonable serving portion.

3 oz portion	kcal	kJ
Cooked stewing steak	189	791
Roast chicken	126	527
Ham	231	967
Kidney	78	326
Roast lamb	249	1042
Grilled liver	140	586
Luncheon meat	270	1130
Roast pork	282	1181
Cod, haddock, other white fish	120	502
Fish fingers	153	640
Herring	198	829
Salmon, canned	132	553
Sardines, canned	186	778

Calories from Vegetables

Some vegetables have high carbohydrate values and are therefore
high in calories. Others contain very little indeed. The range of
variation in values is demonstrated in the main chart on p. 86
by the fact that parsnips are more than twice as calorific as
green beans, which are in turn three times as calorific as celery.
Looking at the chart below, weight-watchers should start their
shopping lists with vegetables from Groups IV and III below, in
that order, looking out for those starred for vitamin C value and
consulting the seasons chart, which you will find on pp. 146–51,
for fresh vegetables.

Group I: most carbohydrate

*Potatoes   Dried or canned peas
*Sweet potatoes   Butter beans or haricot beans
                                 Baked beans

These are all good foods and will suit members of the family who
need plenty of energy food. If the meal also contains much un-
avoidable refined carbohydrate, older people and weight-
watchers should be careful not to eat too much of these items.

Group II: less carbohydrate

Broad beans   *Green peas
Beetroot   Parsnips

These are middle-of-the-road as regards energy value, not as high
as Group I.

Group III: even less carbohydrate

*Brussels sprouts   Onions
 Carrots   Swedes
 Leeks   *Turnips

Most slimming diets include these foods in moderate amounts.

Group IV: only a little carbohydrate

*French beans   Courgettes
*Runner beans   Marrow

*Cabbage   Mushrooms
*Cauliflower   *Spring greens
*Broccoli tops   *Turnip tops
 Celery   *Peppers
 Chicory   *Radishes
 Endive   *Watercress
 Lettuce   *Mustard and cress

Best buys for slimmers, widely used in reducing diets and good for anyone else in ordinary meals.

Finally, it is important to remember that any vegetable fried or served with butter or other fat will be very much higher in calories than if it is cooked some other way and served plain. To make vegetables more appetizing use a squeeze of lemon juice plus black pepper or homemade sesame seed salt.

Calories from Fruits

When weight-watchers look at a more detailed fruit list the first choice should always be the low-calorie fruits which can be eaten raw without any additional sweetening:

Apricots   Pears
Melons   Plums
Oranges   Tangerines
Peaches

Then there are the low-carbohydrate fruits generally eaten with sugar and cream. To enjoy these without all the extra calories we need to get back to remembering how good they tasted when we ate them straight from the bushes. They are all improved by warming on a dish in the sun for a short time before serving:

Strawberries   Blackberries
Raspberries

Now consider the fruits usually stewed with sugar. The only hope for weight-watchers here is to use an artificial sweetener:

Blackcurrants	Rhubarb
Gooseberries	Cooking apples
Redcurrants	

The following fruits contain more calories, but can be eaten sometimes by slimmers:

Apples	Figs
Bananas	Greengages
Grapes	Pineapple
Nectarines	Damsons
Cherries	

Canned fruits are very high in calories compared with fresh fruits. The carbohydrate value is often doubled by the large amounts of sugar used in heavy syrups.

Dried fruits are concentrated in all nutrients, including sugars, but they are only a danger for people with a tendency to overweight who are addicted to nibbling them in quantity. Otherwise they are good for natural flavouring or sweetening and for providing minerals.

Calories from High-fat Foods

Fat is the most concentrated source of calories. If the amount of fat we eat is greater than 30 per cent of the total calories in our meal, we will inevitably be involved in a life-long struggle to keep our weight down. A glance at the chart on p. 69 will explain the problem.

EATING OUT

Restaurant menus often tempt people to overeat on the grounds that they are 'paying so much for it anyway' and 'it's a special occasion'. With business entertaining there is sometimes an added incentive to have a feast because someone else is footing the bill.

An excellent plan of campaign in a restaurant is to choose a starter from the vegetable section, bypassing the rich pâtés, hors d'oeuvres with mayonnaise and thick soups. Choose instead asparagus (with lemon, not butter), an artichoke, braised celery, haricots verts or a tomato salad. Waiters ladle salad dressings on generously. To control the amount you have to serve yourself.

Then you can proceed to the main course in the French style, enjoying it with its own garnish and perhaps a green salad. There's no need to order three extra vegetables and turn it into a plateful of dinner fit for a farm worker—unless you happen to be a farm worker, in which case the meal you choose has to supply a lot of energy to compensate for that expended in heavy manual work. If the meal is French, a roast of meat may be accompanied by a dish of white haricot beans, peas or a lentil purée, in which case you will have chosen a meal with good fibre content.

Most of us expect to have a treat in a restaurant, so we look for exotic wine and cream sauces. It is often a pleasant surprise to see how beautifully the simpler dishes are cooked, served and garnished, and how much fitter one feels after them.

With fish dishes choose grilled plaice or sole, cod baked with tomatoes and onions or peppers, smoked mackerel, scallops or curried fish salads.

The cheese board can be as much of a hazard as the sweet trolley. A creamy French cheese with biscuits and butter is very high in calories.

8. Vitamins and Minerals in the Shopping Basket

Up till now we have been thinking about protein, carbohydrates and fats, all nutrients which are eaten in comparatively large quantities. With vitamins and minerals, the amounts required are small, sometimes very small indeed, yet they are absolutely essential.

VITAMINS

These can be thought of as catalysts or trigger substances which make it possible for all the complicated chemical reactions to proceed in the body as food is used to build and repair body tissues, provide warmth and energy, and protect health. Before this century it was thought that so long as food gave enough protein, carbohydrate, fat and minerals everything was all right. It has now been shown that there are certain complex organic substances, occurring naturally in foods, in very small amounts, which are vital for health. These are called vitamins.

For example, as one type of amino acid changes into another a trigger is needed to make the necessary chemical reaction happen. If the trigger is missing, the action comes to a halt and the planned chain of reactions cannot continue. These triggers are the vitamins.

It is quite usual to explain the function of a particular vitamin by describing what happens if that vitamin is completely missing from the diet. In practice, of course, a diet missing one vitamin may be missing several others as well, but it has been shown, by some extreme cases of deficiency, that severe illnesses can be caused by the absence from meals of one particular vitamin. For example:

Without vitamin C: During long voyages sailors who had no fresh fruit and vegetables used to suffer from scurvy. Many died from this disease, the earlier symptoms of which were weakness, listlessness, swelling and bleeding of the gums, bleeding under the skin and the failure of wounds to heal.

Without vitamin D: Poorly nourished children in industrial towns in the United Kingdom used to suffer from rickets, because the development of bones and teeth was hampered.

Without vitamin A: During the First World War, Danish children suffered from keratomalacia, a soreness of the eyes sometimes leading to blindness. This was because their home consumption of dairy produce was greatly reduced due to so much being exported.

Without vitamin B_1: A disease called beri-beri killed thousands of people in Africa and Asia when the refining of rice and wheat was first introduced. At that time there was no replacement of the vitamins removed by the milling process.

At first sight these descriptions of illnesses caused by vitamin deficiencies seem irrelevant to us because they are such extreme cases. They are the dramatic results of having almost none of a particular vitamin over a period of time. But if we have a little of the vitamin but not enough of it, lesser adverse effects will occur, and these can be unpleasant and lowering to general health.

For each vitamin there is an amount needed to prevent serious illness, an amount on which one can get by reasonably well, and an amount on which the body can function at its best. The purpose of applied nutrition is not just to prevent illness but to provide for optimum health and wellbeing. One of the most complicated facts about nutrition is that each individual has different needs for all the various nutrients. It is only possible to generalize by saying, for example, that if you are an adult man of a given height and weight you are *likely* to need X mg of a certain vitamin each day.

Some vitamins can be stored in the body if extra is taken on a particular day. Many others cannot be stored but are constantly eliminated from the body if they are not used. These are the vitamins that dissolve in water: vitamin C and the B vitamins. The vitamins which can be stored are those that dissolve in fat, vitamins A, D, E and K. For this reason it is important to have vitamins B and C every day, but with the others the intake can be higher on some days and lower on others provided that the total is up to the requirement over a period of a few days.

VITAMINS AT A GLANCE

Below is a complete list of vitamins. This information is still very much simplified, however, and should on no account be used for formal study purposes, when an approved textbook must be consulted. The purpose of including this chart is to indicate the wide range of activities which vitamins perform, whilst in no way attempting a detailed discussion.

Fat-soluble vitamins	Function	Source
Vitamin A	Essential for the ability to 'see in the dark' and for the health of eye tissues and skin.	Liver, kidney, butter, margarine, milk, cheese, eggs, carrots, tomatoes, dark green vegetables.
Vitamin D	Helps absorption of calcium from the intestine; regulates calcium entering bones from the blood.	The oily fish, margarine, milk, cheese, eggs and butter.
Vitamin E	Role not clear, but may play a part in fat metabolism, helping to prevent artery trouble.	Vegetable oils which are made from seeds or from cereal grains, other cereal products (particularly wheatgerm), eggs.

Fat-soluble vitamins	*Function*	*Source*
Vitamin K	Needed for normal blood clotting.	Cabbage, cauliflower, spinach, peas, foods produced from cereal grains.

Water-soluble vitamins	*Function*	*Source*
(all except the last are B vitamins)		
Vitamin B_1 (Thiamine)	For release of energy from carbohydrate.	Yeast, liver, kidney, pork, bacon, ham, other meats to a lesser extent, eggs, wholegrain bread and cereals, white bread which by law has added vitamins, enriched breakfast cereals, peas, beans, lentils and nuts.
Vitamin B_2 (Riboflavin)	For utilization of energy from food.	Meat (especially liver), eggs, yeast, milk, wholegrain or enriched cereals and bread.
Nicotinic acid	For utilization of energy from food.	Liver, kidney, other meats, yeast, wholegrain and enriched cereals and bread, oatmeal, peas, beans.
Vitamin B_6 (Pyridoxine)	For metabolism of amino acids and for formation of haemoglobin.	Meat, fish, eggs, wholegrain cereals and bread, green vegetables.

(*see over*)

Water-soluble vitamins	Function	Source
Vitamin B_{12} (Cyanoco-balamin)	Lack of this causes pernicious anaemia.	Liver is a very good source. Also found in eggs, cheese, milk, meat and fish.
Folic acid	Lack of this can cause megaplastic anaemia.	Liver, fish, raw leafy green vegetables, peas, beans and wholemeal bread.
Pantothenic acid	For release of energy from carbohydrate and fat.	Widespread in animal protein foods, also in cereals, peas, beans and many other vegetables.
Biotin	For fat metabolism.	Liver, kidney, egg yolk.
Vitamin C (Ascorbic acid)	For maintenance of healthy connective tissue; also facilitates absorption of iron.	Green vegetables, potatoes, citrus fruits, soft summer berry fruits, and in other fruits and vegetables in smaller amounts.

(*Note:* some of the foods mentioned are very rich sources of the vitamin in question; others are moderate sources; value will also depend on quantity and frequency of eating.)

MINERALS INCLUDING TRACE ELEMENTS

When minerals are mentioned one usually thinks of iron, copper and zinc being mined in large quantities and used in manufacturing a wide range of goods. Although calcium, iron and sodium (as common salt) are not unexpected in our food, many people would be surprised to know that potassium, copper, cobalt, chromium, iodine, fluorine, magnesium, manganese, selenium and zinc all feature in the foodstuffs we buy or grow. These minerals are not present because manufacturers have added them, but because they occur in small quantities as part of the natural make-up of plants and animals. What is more they are needed to keep the chemical processes of the body working; they are therefore essential for our growth, health and energy.

In the opening chapter it was stated that human tissues are made up of cells and that cells consist of chemicals and water. The most important of these chemicals are listed below. It can be seen that all these elements have important roles to play in maintaining health. No one would expect to relate such detailed knowledge to a shopping list, nor would they need to do so. However, the starred items are worthy of more discussion in relation to one's general policy of food choice, and these will be discussed in detail later. Conversely, I am aware that I am oversimplifying the descriptions and in some cases not describing all the functions of a particular mineral. This is a deliberate intention in order to keep the picture simple.

MAJOR MINERAL ELEMENTS, THEIR FUNCTION AND SOURCES

Element	Function	Source
Oxygen, Carbon, Hydrogen, Nitrogen	The basic elements from which our body protein and fat are built.	These basic elements exist as major items in molecules of protein, carbohydrate and fat in foods.
*Calcium, Phosphorus	Very important for the construction of bones and teeth. Calcium and phosphorus are constituents of blood, too, and have roles to play in many metabolic processes.	Calcium: milk, cheese, commercially produced white bread, canned fish where the bones are eaten, green vegetables. Phosphorus: present in most foods.

(see over)

Element	Function	Source
Magnesium	Occurs widely in tissues and bones, and plays an important part in metabolism. If the diet is deficient in magnesium, weakness and depression result.	Present in most foods.
*Sodium	Present in our body as sodium chloride (common salt), this is the most important mineral as it keeps the body fluid environment constant. There are accurate salt-regulating mechanisms.	Present in most foods, but in low amounts unless salt has been added during processing.
Potassium	Similar role to sodium, but whereas sodium is mainly found functioning in fluids like blood and sweat (i.e. fluids outside the cells), potassium regulates the state of fluids inside the cells.	Present in many foods, but vegetables, milk and meat are particularly rich sources.
*Iron	Very important for building haemoglobin, the blood pigment responsible for carrying oxygen. Also in myoglobin, the oxygen-carrying pigment in muscles, and in cytochromes, the respiratory enzymes of many cells.	Meat, especially liver and kidney, eggs, brown and white bread, flour, other cereal products including oats, figs, dried apricots, prunes, black treacle, molasses, cocoa.

TRACE ELEMENTS, THEIR FUNCTION AND SOURCES

Trace element	Function	Source
*Zinc	For building cell proteins from food amino acids, therefore necessary for tissue growth.	Present in most foods.
Copper	A catalyst for essential chemical reactions.	Present in most foods.
Cobalt	An essential part of vitamin B_{12}.	Present in vitamin B_{12} where it occurs in foods.
Manganese	Forms part of certain enzyme systems.	Wholegrain cereals, nuts.
Selenium	Concerned with the activity of vitamin E.	Present in most foods.
Chromium	Needed for fat and sugar metabolism in which insulin takes part. Needed for normal cholesterol metabolism (see Chapter 6).	Present in wholegrain cereal foods, raw sugar, molasses, fruit juices.
Iodine	Part of the thyroid hormone, thyroxine.	Fish, some vegetables and cereal products.
Fluorine	Necessary for strong bones and teeth.	Drinking water, tea.
Molybdenum	Part of an enzyme.	Present in most foods.

D

VITAMINS AND MINERALS ON YOUR FOOD SHOPPING LIST

Most people find it hard to remember much about the exact quantities of different nutrients needed, and in any case it is often difficult to think clearly when one is out shopping. This is where a shopping list is vital. It has to be prepared at home quietly, and you need to decide whether you are going to keep to it exactly or to mark items which you are prepared to be flexible about when you see what is in the shops. Keeping to the list fairly firmly probably results in the most economical shopping, but it is worth being flexible about fresh vegetables and fruit as this is an area of significant price fluctuations.

I keep in mind just a few important minerals and vitamins when I plan shopping lists:

Calcium, because the children need to have enough for growth, elderly people need it to protect their bones, and adults need a 'maintenance' amount each day.

Iron, because the women need more iron than the men and boys in a family.

Vitamin C, because everyone benefits by having some vitamin C in each meal, to be used in a 'cementing' capacity as tissues are built and repaired. Vitamin C also helps us to utilize the iron in our food.

Vitamin B_1, because, as explained in the chapter on carbohydrates, this is the main energy-giving vitamin. Also, foods which are rich in vitamin B_1 often contain many other B vitamins as well. Vitamin B_1 is necessary for appetite and nerve health, too.

Vitamin D, because it is needed by the younger members of the family for the development of bones and teeth. Older people need it too in a repair and maintenance capacity.

When meal patterns are examined closely and notes taken of what people really eat, any one of these essential ingredients for health may turn out to be under-supplied. Individual requirements vary, and one may be counting on a certain food to supply a nutrient, forgetting that one member of the family (and it could be the one who needs it most) never eats much of that kind of food.

Teaching Children About Vitamins and Minerals

It is worth teaching a family all the nutrition they can cope with because it is to everyone's advantage to know how to choose food well. Many families are very keen on sport and health, early nights, fresh air and exercise, academic achievement and sociability, but it seems much less acceptable—'why bother anyway?'—to think seriously about the food which ultimately makes us the way we are.

Quite young children soon learn which foods are for protein and associate milk, eggs and cheese with growing taller. The concepts of vitamins and minerals can be introduced in simple terms as they get older.

Calcium is easy to explain: their milk and cheese provide this.

Vitamin D, the sunshine vitamin, fascinates children because it is a vitamin you can make for yourself if the skin is exposed to sunlight, as it is when they play outdoors in swimsuits in summer.

Iron is easy to learn about as children become young teenagers. By then they have had biology lessons about the blood and its circulation. They know that blood is red because it contains a pigment called haemoglobin and that iron is needed to build this pigment. They also learn that women and girls need extra iron to replace their monthly menstrual losses.

Vitamin B_1 is often described to youngsters as the 'sparking plug' vitamin. Like the sparking plug in a car it triggers the reaction between the fuel (carbohydrate) and oxygen and thus energy is produced.

Vitamin C helps to make the body's cement-like substances, keeping all the tissues strong. It is needed for wounds to heal well and to help us to recover from feverish infections.

CHOOSING FOOD FOR VITAMINS AND MINERALS

We now turn to look at some actual portions of foods, as we are accustomed to seeing them in our kitchens and on our plates. Having taught the basic principles of nutrition, the next thing is to teach how to buy nutrition and how to select meals in a canteen, dining-room, snack bar or wherever there is a degree of choice. For food choosers it is helpful to know something about quantities of foods which make a significant contribution to our vitamin and mineral requirements.

The foods chosen for the charts are ones which in the reasonable portions shown are able to make a significant contribution to our daily requirements of the particular vitamin or mineral. Other foods will make smaller and still useful contributions and may be used in place of some of those shown. A book of food value tables must be consulted if the reader wishes to pursue the matter in more depth.

Portions of Food Supplying One-sixth of the Iron Needed by Adults

This is based on the recommended adult allowance of 12 mg iron each day. Adults need 6 portions; young people, pregnant and nursing mothers need $7\frac{1}{2}$ portions; children aged three to seven need 4 portions, and children aged seven to nine need 5 portions.

4 oz (115 g) roast or casseroled beef or lamb*
$2\frac{1}{2}$ oz (75 g) corned beef
4 oz (115 g) beefburgers, one large or two small
5 oz (140 g) beef sausages
7 oz (200 g) pork sausages
1 oz (30 g) cooked liver
$2\frac{1}{2}$ oz (75 g) canned sardines, about four
1 egg with 2 oz (60 g) slice shortback bacon

* Chicken and pork have much lower iron values than beef and lamb

3 oz (90 g) portion of baked beans on a slice of toast
2¼ oz (65 g) wholemeal bread, 2 small slices
1½–2 oz (45–60 g) oatmeal as porridge
2 wholewheat cereal biscuits
2 shredded wheat cereal biscuits
1 portion of muesli
1 oz (30 g) wheatgerm
1½ oz (45 g) dried beans
2 oz (60 g) dried figs, apricots, prunes
2 oz (60 g) peanuts, almonds

Portions of Food Supplying a Quarter of the Calcium Needed Each Day for Children, Young People and Adults

This is based on an allowance of 600 mg per day. The recommended allowances are 600 mg calcium each day for girls and boys aged fifteen to eighteen, 500 mg for adults and 1,200 mg during pregnancy and breastfeeding.

Each day choose 4 portions from the main list or 3 portions plus some foods from the additional list.

¼ pint (150 ml) milk
Another ¼ pint (150 ml), because ½ pint (300 ml) is a sensible amount of milk to drink each day.
⅔ oz (18 g) cheese, Cheddar or other hard cheese, a 2 cm cube
1 small herring or mackerel
2 or 3 sardines
1 oz (30 g) serving of boiled spinach

Additional list of good, but less concentrated sources of calcium:

Other cheeses
Eggs
White fish
Canned salmon and tuna fish
Cabbage
Turnips

Foods Supplying Vitamin D in Normal Everyday Meals

Milk	Herrings
Cheese	Mackerel
Margarine	Salmon
Eggs	Sardines
Butter	Tuna

It is difficult to recommend precise portions for this vitamin, but important that these foods are well represented in our meals.

For infants and children under 6 vitamin D supplements are given, in amounts strictly governed by advice from a doctor or child health clinic.

For older children the requirement is covered if they drink their milk regularly and have eggs, cheese and butter or margarine frequently, plus a serving of one of the oily fish each week.

Vitamin D is also made in the skin when exposed to sunlight, so that in hot climates people wearing almost no clothes do not need to rely on food for this vitamin. On the other hand, in recent years some Asian children living in Britain have developed mild rickets, due to wearing a lot of clothes and being unaware that foods for vitamin D are needed in our climate.

Portions of Foods Supplying Vitamin B₁

The individual requirement of this vitamin is related to the amount of carbohydrate eaten. The requirement for men is highest, about 1·2 mg each day. 6 portions each day supply the requirements for men and older boys; 5 portions each day for women and girls, and 4 portions each day for children of five to eight years.

$1\frac{1}{2}$ oz (45 g) muesli
3 oz (90 g) wholemeal bread
1 oz (30 g) wheatgerm, 1 well-heaped tablespoon
2 oz (60 g) grilled bacon
2 oz (60 g) ham, 1 large thin slice
1 oz (30 g) luncheon meat, 1 slice

$1\frac{1}{2}$ oz (45 g) lean pork
3 oz (90 g) liver, 2 small slices
3 oz (90 g) fresh or frozen peas
$2\frac{1}{2}$ oz (75 g) broad beans
2 oz (60 g) dried peas
$1\frac{1}{2}$ oz (45 g) haricot beans, butter beans or lentils
1 oz (30 g) plain peanuts or Brazil nuts (roasting diminishes vitamin B_1)
2 oz (60 g) almonds

Vitamin B_1 is often given, together with other B vitamins, to treat people suffering from lack of appetite and general apathy. Quite dramatic improvements have been made with elderly patients when vitamin B therapy has been followed by a vitamin B-rich diet.

Other foods which are quite good for vitamin B_1 are listed below, so if you choose less than the required number of portions from the main list you are likely to make up the rest by including these foods often in your meal plans:

Fish
Potatoes
Eggs
Green vegetables
Apples

Portions of Food Giving at Least Half the Day's Requirement of Vitamin C, Based on a Daily Requirement of 30 mg

Choose at least 2 portions a day.

1 oz (30 g) orange, half a small orange is more than enough
$1\frac{1}{2}$ oz (45 g) grapefruit, a quarter of a small grapefruit
2 oz (60 g) melon, 1 slice
5 oz (140 g) banana, 1 medium
2 oz (60 g) gooseberries or raspberries
1 oz (30 g) strawberries
$\frac{1}{2}$ oz (15 g) blackcurrants, carefully cooked

(see over)

2 fl oz (60 ml) orange juice, grapefruit juice or tomato juice
⅓ fl oz (10 ml) rosehip syrup, e.g. poured over fruit salad
1 fl oz (30 ml) lemon juice
1 fl oz (30 ml) blackcurrant syrup

1 oz (30 g) watercress
2½ oz (75 g) tomato
½ oz (15 g) green pepper
3 oz (90 g) runner beans
2½ oz (75 g) peas, fresh or frozen
2 oz (60 g) cauliflower, cooked
1 oz (30 g) cabbage, raw shredded
3 oz (90 g) cabbage, cooked 5 minutes, served at once
5 oz (140 g) cabbage, cooked 30 minutes
1½ oz (45 g) Brussels sprouts, cooked
2 oz (60 g) new potatoes
8 oz (225 g) old potatoes
10 oz (280 g) French fried potatoes

FURTHER FACTS ABOUT VITAMIN C

Vitamin C is the vitamin most often inadequately represented in meals. It is essential for the following reasons:

a. For making cement-like substances which hold together the body's cells. Adequate vitamin C ensures that children's bones, teeth, blood vessels and skin develop really beautifully. For adults it is the key to strong bones and teeth, resistance to infection and quick wound-healing.
b. For helping the body to absorb iron, the great anaemia-preventer. Iron and vitamin C must go together. They are important in every day's meals.

Efforts have also been made to substantiate the claim that vitamin C helps prevent colds. So far this has not been proved, but many people find that vitamin C does help fight cold symptoms. We know it is associated with tissue health and is used in connection with wound-healing after operations, including dental extractions. Perhaps we shall find in due course that its chief value for the common cold lies in helping to prevent the secondary infections that so often follow.

When Buying Foods that are Rich in Vitamin C

—If budgeting carefully, choose potatoes, cabbage, spinach, watercress, oranges, canned tomatoes and frozen peas.

—If you have a little more to spend, and at the seasonal times of year for each item, choose grapefruits, lemons, fresh tomatoes, green beans, cauliflower, Brussels sprouts, green peppers and soft fruit such as raspberries, strawberries and blackcurrants. Quite small portions of the soft fruits mentioned give the necessary amount of vitamin C, so a strawberry shortcake, blackcurrant crumble or raspberries made into 'freezer jam' will make the vitamin C food go further. On pp. 146–51 there is a practical section on buying 'vitamin C value' right through the year.

—Notice in the vitamin C-portions chart that comparatively small glasses of fruit juice give good supplies of vitamin C. Give small glasses of breakfast orange juice, or share a grapefruit, segmenting it like an orange. One grapefruit between four people is a healthy and sociable way to start the day.

When Cooking Foods Rich in Vitamin C
Remember that:

Vitamin C dissolves very easily in water so it can be washed away from the cut surfaces of fruit and vegetables when they are cooked in water. The less we chop fruit and vegetables before cooking, the less water we cook in, and the shorter the cooking time, the better the vitamin C value remains.

Vitamin C is gradually destroyed by heat, so quick serving is the golden rule. Vitamin C foods are wasted if they are included in meals that have to be kept hot for a period of time. It is better to serve a platter of raw vegetable pieces, which look attractive and taste delicious. The French call them crudités.

Vitamin C is gradually diminished when vegetables are stored particularly when they become flabby and wilted. Thus new potatoes have a higher vitamin C value than old ones (although potatoes remain a useful food for vitamin C throughout the winter). Green vegetables should be used soon after purchasing. Frozen vegetables keep about 70 per cent of their vitamin C, so provided they are carefully cooked according to exact instructions they are a very good choice. For many years potatoes have been one of our main sources of vitamin C. To keep the vitamins in your potato the best method is to cook and eat it complete with the skin, whether baked, boiled or roasted.

Vitamin C is not much stored in the body, so we need to take in vitamin C often. The level circulating in the bloodstream, and therefore quickly available to the cells and tissues, is kept high if it is taken several times a day. One large dose first thing in the morning is unlikely to be as effective as smaller amounts taken in meals throughout the day. This is because the body continually excretes what it does not need of this vitamin.

SODIUM

We usually think of sodium in its most common form, as sodium chloride in common salt. Sodium does, however, occur in foods in other forms, so even without added salt our food may already have a high sodium content. Foods quite high in sodium are milk, cheese, meat, fish and eggs. Vegetables, breads and cereals contain moderate amounts, fruit and fats low amounts.

The adult body is thought to use only about $\frac{1}{2}$ g sodium each day. The recommended amount is 3 g per day, but it has been found in the USA that people are eating double and up to six times this amount. Much of this is hidden in processed foods and masked by other flavourings. Concern has been expressed because those who are predisposed to hypertension (high blood pressure) can have the condition precipitated by a high amount of salt in the diet. Connections have also been suggested between a high sodium intake and heart disease, gastric acid secretion, stomach cancer, cerebrovascular disease and migraine. (In the case of migraine, sufferers are recommended to avoid extra table salt and foods containing monosodium glutamate and sodium nitrite.) The suggested 3 g of salt per day amounts to three-fifths of a teaspoon, and this of course includes the salt in foods.

To moderate our sodium intake we should:

—Avoid highly salted snack foods.
—Halve the amount of salt we use in cooking and at the table.
—Avoid adding salt to foods which have already been salted in canning or freezing.

It is important to remember that we are here considering salt intake in normal circumstances and at normal temperatures. We need more in very hot weather. It is well known that salt is lost in sweat. (In the case of men doing very heavy physical work in a hot climate, losses as great as 14 g per day have been recorded.) The loss, whatever its size, needs replacing, and for this reason the salt requirement increases.

ZINC

This occurs in traces in most foods and is needed in connection with building tissue protein from amino acids. A similar substance, cadmium, is also present in small quantities in our food. A problem arises if the cadmium content of our food is increased and the zinc content decreased, because then cadmium can be absorbed into the kidneys, liver and arteries in place of zinc. The chemical reactions which require zinc will not accept cadmium as a substitute, so certain metabolic reactions are prevented, and the results of this may contribute to high blood pressure.

Factors which raise our cadmium intakes are:

a. Foods high in cadmium and low in zinc.
b. Cigarette smoking.
c. Drinking water containing cadmium. Water which a water board has passed as safe may pick up extra cadmium from domestic water pipes.
d. Air pollution which can cause cadmium to be absorbed.

We can do little to alleviate the problems of c and d, but we can obviously give up smoking, and in the realm of food choice we can take certain preventive action.

Once again the wholegrain foods are the ones that come out right, with high zinc and low cadmium values. More of the zinc, which we do need, is contained in the brown parts of grains, whilst the cadmium, which we do not need, is firmly embedded in the white part of each grain. Thus, in yet another instance, the refining of grains tends to upset the natural balance of foods.

VITAMIN B_6

This vitamin has never been regarded as important enough to think about when planning shopping lists, but recently it has aroused interest because it has been found that if monkeys are kept short of it they develop lesions in their artery walls similar to the lesions which human beings get in atherosclerosis. It is also known that vitamin B_6 is important as part of an enzyme which makes it possible for food amino acids to be converted into tissue amino acids, and it has been found to be essential for the smoothness of human artery walls and for the health of our nerves.

The exact requirement for an individual cannot be specified, but it would seem wise for everyone, and particularly older people, to make sure that they have plenty of this vitamin. Its importance is neglected because it is widely distributed in many foods, especially in:

—Liver, other meats, green vegetables: *but* cooking partially destroys vitamin B_6.
—Wholegrain cereals, flour products: *but* refining grains and flour removes vitamin B_6.
—Milk: *but* pasteurization depletes vitamin B_6.

Some older people base their meals on white bread and butter. Living alone they seldom cook meat and sometimes do not even bother with fresh vegetables, preferring to open a can of baked beans. One of the things they may be short of is vitamin B_6.

Usually they will be short of several other ingredients for health at the same time, but there is reason to believe that shortage of vitamin B_6 may be the direct cause of insomnia and soreness at the sides of the mouth as well as the artery and nerve effects. So although this is not a vitamin to think about supplying in a specific amount, it is nevertheless another good reason for including unrefined cereals and flour products in one's diet.

Good Food Choice at a Glance

PROTEIN-RICH FOODS FOR MAIN COURSES

	Food	Why?
A good choice at any time	Fish, chicken, turkey	Fish and poultry are lower in total fat content than meat, and fish contains unsaturated oils.
	Dried peas, beans, lentils	Using some vegetable proteins to supplement or replace animal proteins.
A good choice sometimes	Lean beef, veal, pork, lamb	Good for iron and B vitamins. Choose lean meat, remove fat.
	Eggs	Good for iron but not to be eaten in great numbers because of cholesterol content.
	Cheese, hard ones preferably, soft ones occasionally	Hard cheeses have lowest fat, cholesterol and calorie values.
A good choice sometimes	Liver, kidney, not more than once a week	Good for iron and B vitamins, but too high in cholesterol to eat frequently.

	Food	*Why?*
What is not so good	Large-sized portions of meat	These give us excess calories and fat.
	Sausages and bacon	Because of the high fat content. Grill to reduce fat and choose lean boiled ham.
	Meat or fish fried in batter	Because of high fat and calorie content.
	Canned or sliced cold meats	Because of the high salt and preservative content. It is better to cook extra when you buy a joint and use this for cold meals.
	Pâtés, salted or smoked meat or fish	Because of high fat and salt content.

MILK PRODUCTS

A good choice	Whole milk 1 pint (600 ml) a day for children, ½ pint (300 ml) for adults, skimmed milk, non-fat dried milk, yoghurt made with skimmed milk, cottage cheese	These are the dairy products with the lowest fat content and the lowest calories. See p. 74 concerning use of skimmed milk.
What to cut down	Cream, sour cream, cream cheese, butter, icecream	These are high-fat products.

Breads, Cereals and Starchy Vegetables

	Food	*Why?*
A good choice	Wholemeal bread and cereal, oatmeal, rice and pasta (preferably brown), other grains	Carbohydrate foods richest in natural vitamins, minerals and fibre. Also containing some protein.
	Starchy vegetables such as potatoes, peas and sweetcorn	Good for supplying complex carbohydrate at low cost. Also rich in minerals and vitamins and containing some protein.
	Cakes, biscuits and pastries made with wholemeal flour or flour of 81–85 per cent extraction, nuts, vegetable oil, dried fruit	Tasty and satisfying in small portions. No saturated fats used. Flavouring from fruit and nuts rather than sugar.
What to cut down	Sugar-coated breakfast cereals	Too much sugar and too 'more-ish'. Changing to a plainer cereal is more satisfying.
	Most cakes, biscuits, pies and puddings	High fat and sugar content.

OTHER VEGETABLES

	Food	*Why?*
A good choice	All vegetables, at least half of them to be eaten raw	Good for vitamins, minerals and fibre.
What to cut down	Deep frying of vegetables, cream sauces with vegetables, generous butter glazes	These each give too much fat, and too many calories.
	Too much salt in cooking.	Too much salt can be bad for you.

PUDDINGS

The best choices	Fresh and dried fruit Unsweetened canned and frozen fruit Puddings made with skimmed milk Brown flour fruit crumbles with a low proportion of fat and sugar
The worst choices	Puddings containing a lot of fat and sugar Pastries, buns and doughnuts, with high fat and sugar content Most cakes, for the same reason, and iced cakes in particular The richest icecreams

SNACKS

The best choice	A few roasted nuts
The worst choices	Potato snacks, crisps, etc. because of the high fat and salt content, plus the flavourings and preservatives

PART TWO

9. Jungle Territories

The territory of the Food Choice Jungle is varied. Starting with the frozen north of the big freezer centres, all ice and efficiency, we move southwards to find airy supermarkets where the going is comparatively easy. Smaller self-service shops and speciality shops usually have pleasant friendly inhabitants, and here the art of conversation is still practised. In some places local street markets are set up once or twice a week. In remote parts you may find a lone itinerant man running a mobile shop: in even more isolated regions the 'bush telegraph' signals to mail-order suppliers that stocks are running low.

Basic principles of retailing apply wherever food is sold. The retailer provides this service:

a. He buys in bulk and sells to us in the smaller quantities which we find convenient.
b. He uses space to hold supplies in readiness for our shopping excursions.
c. He holds these supplies in a place which we find convenient to visit.

Some retailers sell everything under one roof. Others specialize in meat, fish, vegetables or baked goods and offer more personal service. We can choose where to shop. Shall we go to small local shops or to town centres, where the convenience of shopping precincts is offset by the cost of car parking? Is it worth driving a bit further to an out-of-town shopping centre where there is free parking?

SELF-SERVICE SHOPS

Wherever we shop nowadays there is an increasing likelihood that we will find a self-service system. This saves paying for extra staff. Changing a counter-service shop into a self-service shop increases the amount of space for the display of goods. The psychologists have been watching the effects of self-service on shopping habits, and they have found that people tend to buy twice as much in a self-service shop as they do in one where they have to ask for each item. Apparently if you can see and touch, lift up and look at goods, your desire to buy them increases and you tend to buy more.

SUPERMARKETS

Many people dislike the idea of food being produced by commercial methods and sold in bulk at vast stores, but this way of providing a wide variety of food has developed to suit modern life in a predominantly industrial society.

Nowadays many housewives are also wage-earners, so their time for shopping is limited to lunch hours or evenings. One-stop shopping at a supermarket or self-service shop is obviously the best solution to the problem. Choosing food which takes less time to prepare will also be important. A supermarket aims to be able to supply everything on a normal household shopping list: groceries, fresh meat, fruit and vegetables, dairy products, frozen food, soaps, other cleaning materials and certain other non-food items.

As with all big businesses there are certain policies behind the running of supermarkets which are fairly general:

a. Having a very wide range of goods available for self-service, with payment to be made at checkouts.
b. Bulk buying to keep costs down. With enormous orders special prices can be negotiated with food manufacturers, who would each prefer to see large quantities of their particular brand in the shops rather than let the order go to a competitor.

c. Low-cost methods. In a small shop someone who is really skilled at selling may have to spend 75 per cent of his or her time unpacking goods and stocking up the shelves. In super-markets forklift trucks can be used for unloading vans, machinery for packaging and conveyor belts for much of the behind-scenes handling. This means that less staff are needed and costs are therefore lower. Shelf-stocking is done as a separate skilled job. One of the most important things is to have really good staff at the checkouts. Often the girl who takes the money is the only point of customer contact and the assistant's attitude can make or mar the feelings of the shoppers.

d. Late-night shopping, which is convenient for customers. Some supermarkets reckon to do 10 per cent of their trade between 6 p.m. and 8 p.m. on Thursday or Friday evenings.

e. Freshness of goods and general cleanliness, essential features from the shopper's point of view, as well as helping the business to run efficiently.

f. High-volume sales at low margins of profit. This technical concept is better explained by the American expression 'Stack it high and sell it cheap'. Provided that there is no shortage of space, mass displays of goods piled in the window, coupled with an advertisement of low prices, create an image of economy and draw the customers.

g. Selective price-cutting. It sounds as though the shop would lose out, but in fact any losses are compensated for. Publicity about price-cuts draws in customers. Most of them, once in the shop, will make a few impulse buys as well as purchasing the bargains they originally wanted.

h. Stocking a range of non-food items, on which there is a higher margin of profit than on foods. This helps to make the shop a financial success.

SUPERMARKETS STUDY CUSTOMERS

Many people may not be aware that because supermarketing is a very complex method of retailing our shopping habits have been thoroughly studied. When you walk into a supermarket, although you may only speak to the checkout assistant, the management know quite a lot about what you are likely to do. They know that some of us like to shop fast, so they provide express checkouts for those buying only a few items. Some like to take their time, and that's fine too because there is no order of 'being served' in a self-service set-up. But slow shoppers can be speeded up, and this will help the management at peak hours when the shop gets crowded. In some shops they do it with music: lively tunes to get us moving quickly at peak times and gentle, relaxing music when business is slack, so that customers will take their time and perhaps consider buying a few more items while it's 'nice and quiet'.

Supermarkets know we are most likely to notice the eye-level shelves, so these are the chosen places for the best-selling lines and for promotions. Have a look next time you are shopping and see if you can spot what they are hoping to encourage you to buy. And if you are looking for a can of peas, which is the British people's favourite canned vegetable, you will probably find it at the far end of the vegetable section as you approach it; this way the management will make sure you notice all the other vegetables as well, and you may be inspired to buy something extra. It has been said that 70 per cent of decisions about what to purchase are made in the stores rather than beforehand.

As you walk around the store you will become part of what is known as 'customer flow'. There are always some people pushing their trolleys against the tide, but by and large the management know which way the greatest number of shoppers is going to flow and this enables them to display goods to the best advantage. As you turn into a shopping lane you may notice in the distance a large wire basket of goods for sale. These are called 'dumps', and they often contain special offers, though not always. By the time you get to it you will have seen a lot of people stop to take an item out of the 'dump'—and maybe an assistant filling it up. So the messages flow through your subconscious mind: 'They usually put bargains there—everyone's buying them—look how quickly they are having to restock!' Just think how much less interested you would have been if you had come upon it suddenly causing congestion in a corner!

Similarly, if you find yourself standing still you may have arrived at what is known as a 'hot spot'. This is a trade name given to a place where you are very likely to buy something extra —like chocolates or sweets at the checkout. Incidentally, this is also often the place chosen to sell razor blades, as they are an item often forgotten in shopping lists.

Obviously making a shopping list and sticking to it is one's only protection against overspending in these circumstances. I realize this all the more as I follow to the checkout a lady with a high-piled trolley and see her looking at the list of what she came in for: 'Detergent, Cigarettes, Something for supper'.

The Advantages of Supermarket Shopping

Behind the scenes in a well-run supermarket, a branch of one of the largest supermarket chains, I discovered how many advantages I am buying when I shop at this store. The shops in this group aim to be: the best rather than the biggest; to have good design for every pack; to have all goods on display until 5.30 p.m. Freshness and quality are the keynotes.

Freshness is ensured by careful date-stamp labelling and by accurate control of the temperatures at which perishable food is prepared, packed and transported. Small shops cannot justify the daily delivery of fresh pies and sausages, which is common practice at larger stores. Handling very large volumes of each product makes it possible to choose the best ways of buying wholesale, in some cases even taking the whole of the produce of certain farms. Some meats are brought in ready butchered and prepacked; many others, which look their best for only a short time after cutting, are butchered on the premises.

These stores use highly sophisticated methods of stock control. A stock-control machine is wheeled around the store and the operator uses a light pen to scan the bar codes on the shelves which need replenishing. Thus the machine automatically registers the stock needed. Back behind the scenes the machine transmits its order to the national headquarters at 5.30 p.m. Messages are teletyped to the appropriate depots and by 7.30 a.m. the next morning the goods are on the shelves, ready for opening time. Lorries have driven in from several depots in the very early morning to deliver the goods.

It is not hard to provide high quality at high prices but a good supermarket aims to combine high quality with competitive prices. A really large organization can afford to check the quality by having a team of food technologists who visit suppliers at home and abroad to make sure that they are complying with specifications. These food technologists also work with suppliers in the development of new 'own label' lines. Laboratories and a home economics department provide services to the company in constantly checking the nutritional and microbiological quality of products, especially keeping an eye on new lines. It is a comforting thought that any problem discovered with a single product at one store can, through modern communication techniques, result in the withdrawal of that product within half an hour from the shelves of every branch store in the country.

Knowing all this, one does feel that to shop at a really good supermarket which is part of a big organization is to gain considerable advantages.

TOWN MARKETS

A hundred years ago these were the main shopping centres in Britain, as they are today in developing countries. Traditional market days are still popular and well supported by customers who want to take advantage of lower prices and some farm produce.

The main feature of market selling is that the overheads are low compared with those of shops. In fine weather working in a market is no problem, but in bad weather stallholders have to put up with the fact that theirs is a semi-outdoor job. Nevertheless, by accepting this they are able to offer goods at lower prices and still make a good profit. It is quite usual to be able to do most of one's shopping in a market. Only in the field of groceries do stallholders find it difficult to compete with the bulk purchasing power of larger shops.

Some stallholders will be local farmers trading in fresh country produce; their stalls will be very good for 'in-season' vegetables and fruit, but in order to make a go of such a stall they have to provide variety. So we need to watch the prices and quality of their imported extras, such as oranges and tomatoes. Their stalls of farm eggs, dairy produce and country sausages are always a joy, however, and a change from buying everything date-stamped and plastic-wrapped.

Apart from local traders, many of the others are likely to be itinerant salespeople who travel from town to town. They ply their wares at different markets, thus making their living as full-time retailers with low overhead costs.

Bargains there will always be, particularly at certain times, such as late on Saturday afternoons, when whole crates of produce may be sold off cheaply. The other side of the coin is that market shopping is definitely not a leisurely activity. It's a case of queuing up and being ready to shout for what you want above the general noise; then being prepared to accept the possibility of variable quality as a reasonable risk taken in the interests of overall economy.

BULK BUYING

This is becoming popular, particularly where groups of people share the purchasing. It is possible to save about 10 per cent on the total food bill by taking advantage of bulk price offers or by negotiating special terms. Points to watch are:

—Quality: is it as good as one wants?
—Cost: payment is made well ahead of actual eating time.
—Cost of storage: extra shelving, cupboards or freezer.

MAIL ORDER

Mail order seems for the most part to be quite an expensive way of buying food nowadays. Catalogue prices have to be compared very carefully with those in the shops. There will be some bargains but transport costs have forced prices up a lot in recent years. Mail order can be used very successfully to purchase certain items in bulk from a country supplier, where you are buying high quality at a normal kind of price. Examples of this are bacon and cheese, successfully sent through the post to stock home freezers.

MOBILE SHOPS

These are popular in rural areas. A large van can be fitted out and driven round out-of-town estates and isolated villages. Their great advantage over retailers is that they are not bound by regulations on 'closing times', so they can operate at times when other shops are not open.

WHOLEFOOD SHOPS

The health-food industry is at its best when shops get down to selling grains, flours, pulses, nuts, seeds and dried fruits by the pound. Prices can be kept low, and when there are price fluctuations the retailer is usually able to give his customers a good 'deal'. Often the increase in price of one commodity may be offset by a drop in the price of another similar one. Wholefood shops provide the opportunity to buy great variety in beans and nuts, for example, whereas other shops confine their stocks of these items to a few favourite lines sold in packages. The variety in lentils alone is worth exploring.

This is also the place to look for biscuits made with nutritious ingredients, and fruit and nut bars as an alternative to sweets for children. Often trying an expertly ready-made product of an unusual type will encourage a customer to buy a recipe book and ingredients on the next visit. The plain muesli bases, which are mixtures of rolled grains, are always available, together with good-quality dried fruits, including plump seedless raisins and figs. Herbs and spices are good too, often sold by the ounce.

These shops are not by any means just for vegetarians. Everyone who is interested in basic, wholesome, unprocessed foods will need to shop sometimes in a wholefood shop. It is a myth that such food is expensive. There are inevitably many elaborate mixtures and manufactured foods in these shops, as in all others. There are also some foods specially suited to people with allergies and dietary problems of a medical nature. But many young people, working to a strict budget, bypass the convenience foods and purchase wholefood products from these stores, and live very well on largely vegetarian food.

We have now looked at different types of food merchants in some of their many market places. Personal choice will depend on circumstances and one's nature. Perhaps, as I do, you will try to combine the best features of all of them, splitting up the shopping list accordingly.

10. Paths through the Jungle

The first section of this book has set out to show what our nutritional needs are. (A summary of what we have learned is given on pp. 112–15.) But although it is quite easy to work out scientifically what people need to eat each day, people come in all shapes, sizes and lifestyles. Their likes, dislikes and set ideas are the major obstacles to changing for the better as far as food choice is concerned. For the most part nutritionists can only tell us what is good for us; the actual choosing and eating is up to the individual.

Psychologists say that we cling very firmly to our habits regarding food. If knowledge of nutrition shows up some poor features in our personal eating habits it is best to think in terms of changing slowly because the most successful changes are small ones, with overall change taking place gradually. People frequently decide to change to:

a. Less sugar.
b. More poly-unsaturated fats and less saturated fats, with less total fats as an additional goal.
c. Foods containing more fibre.
d. Eating half of their vegetables raw.

One good change can help another. Each of these changes would benefit health. Each might be tackled separately and slowly. But a and c could be linked, as eating more bulky, fibre-containing carbohydrate foods reduces the 'peckish' feelings that make us reach for sweet things. Similarly, if you begin to eat some vegetables raw, chopped or grated as salads, you discover a delicious range of salad dressings based on oil and vinegar. Thus the oil replaces the butter often put on to cooked vegetables. So in achieving d, work is also begun on b. Incidentally, an oil and black pepper dressing can be used on cooked vegetables too in place of butter. Notice how d also contributes to c.

WHAT IS AVAILABLE?

In the process of constantly craving for something different it is possible to overlook the simplest way of creating variety, namely by having a repertoire of recipes for different ways of serving the most basic of 'in-season' foods. For inspiration of this kind look, for example, at the English version of *Larousse Gastronomique,* available through local libraries. Here you will find 108 ways to cook potatoes, twenty carrot dishes, ten herring recipes and about 390 ideas for eggs! You may not have a wide range of subsidiary ingredients, but there will be many ideas which are easy to use. The same is true in hunting for recipes for using most basic foods.

Having a variety of ways of serving a limited range of simple but very good basic commodities is the philosophy behind much of the world's best country cooking. Working in this way one shops for a smaller range of good-quality foods. Less time is spent shopping, as vast lists of unusual items make shopping harder work than it need be. This is where the idea of 'ever-readies' comes into its own.

Ever-readies, the Foods that Simplify Catering
Ever-readies are foods selected for their good nutritional value, versatility and ease of storage. It is possible to make a whole day's meals from them in an emergency, or to use them to supplement a meal that is too small, but their main use is as the backbone of a catering plan where the aim is good food value at low cost. These are the foods to have always available, our answer to the challenge of 'instant foods'. Most of the foods listed on the following page keep well in a cool, dry place and make a very good basic store. Those vegetables marked * are versatile and inexpensive and store well.

Ever-readies

Wholemeal flour

Dried yeast

Good bread

Brown rice and pasta

Rolled oats

Nuts

Wheatgerm

Lentils, split peas and beans

Dried fruits

Margarine

Peanut butter

Cheese

Dried skimmed milk

Eggs

Yoghurt

Tuna fish, canned

Fruit juices, canned or frozen

Canned tomatoes, oranges
    and grapefruit

Potatoes*

Cabbage*

Carrots*

Turnips*

Onions*

From ever-readies I can make the following:

Breakfast: Orange or grapefruit juice or segments.

Porridge or muesli made with oats, wheatgerm, nuts and dried fruit.

Egg dishes with toast.

Lunch: Soup using a choice of lentils, potatoes, onions and carrots.

Open sandwiches of tuna, eggs, cheese or peanut butter.

Coleslaw, using cabbage or carrot sticks.

Stewed dried fruit or prunes soaked in orange juice.

Tea: Wholemeal bread, yeasted buns or fruit cake.

Dinner: A quiche.

Pizza: wholemeal flour, cheese, canned tomatoes.

Vegetable casserole or risotto, with grated cheese.

Lentil cutlets.

Pasta with tomato and onion sauce or with peanut butter sauce.

A salad.

Yoghurt, egg custard, fruit or cheese if not used in the main course.

This is the sort of food which, when purchased in a wholefood restaurant, beautifully served, is a delight to the eye and to the palate. An additional point in favour of keeping a steady store of ever-readies is that if the person responsible for buying the food is tired, unwell or unable to go shopping, a supply of ever-readies ensures that good meals are still available. Even quite young children could prepare themselves a well-balanced and enjoyable meal from this kind of store cupboard. So often people feel that they do not have the makings of an easy meal readily available.

Keeping up-to-date with this list avoids emergency catering problems. For example, a pizza and salad followed by an orange and yoghurt dessert would make a very acceptable meal for unexpected visitors.

Fish

Fish gives us excellent protein, and the fat it contains is unsaturated. For this reason it is recommended that we eat more fish and less meat. However, the rising cost of the most popular varieties has proved a disincentive to fish-buying, and there is some reluctance to try new varieties. Clearly this is an area in which specific teaching about selection and cooking methods would help many families.

The price of fish can be manageable if some cheaper varieties are purchased, for example mackerel, redfish, saithe or coley, huss, hake, whiting, dabs.

The preparation of fish can be eased by getting the fishmonger to remove skin, head and main bones or by buying frozen fish. For frozen fish the price is higher but there is less wastage in terms of inedible parts, and freshness and quality are more standard.

The cooking of fish can be made more pleasant when foil is used to line grill pans or wrap fish for oven baking. Excellent recipe leaflets are given away in many fish shops, and these provide helpful information about the less-well-known fish.

Most people know when to buy cod, haddock, plaice, sole, salmon and herrings and how to cook them. Below are some ideas for using the more unusual fish which are now coming on to the market. For these it may help to know when they are in season.

E

Fish and season	Characteristics	Recommended cooking methods
Coley or saithe (all the year)	Pinky-grey colour, but turns white on cooking.	Bake, grill in steaks, fry in fillets. Fish curry or kebabs.
Hake (November to August)	White fish with firm texture.	Stuff and bake in oven. Grill or poach. Fish curry or kebabs.
Dabs (September to December)	Similar to plaice but small enough to use a whole one per serving.	Use plaice recipes, but as dabs are smaller take care not to overcook.
Redfish (June to December)	Whole fish looks very fierce—do not be off-put.	Good for baking whole using Mediterranean recipes. Can be filleted for grilling or frying.
Whiting (all the year)	A softer fish, delicate flavour, easy to digest, but the bones can be troublesome for children.	Generally cooked whole, fried, baked or stuffed, but can be filleted.
Mackerel (December to July)	Very firm and filling fish, a beautiful nutty colour with excellent flavour. May also be bought as smoked fillet.	Grilled. Poached in cider or fish stock and served cold. Stuffed and baked.
Huss (rock salmon) (most of the year)	Solid and meaty in texture, pinkish in colour, but turns white on cooking.	Fish stews, curries and kebabs, in which the solid texture is helpful.

Recipes may be obtained from the White Fish Authority.

Poultry

Using the following guidelines about what is in season helps to keep costs lower, whether the poultry is for immediate use or for freezing.

—Chickens and capons are available throughout the year.
—September to January is the season for turkeys.
—January and February is the season for geese.
—March to September is the season for duck.

Chicken and turkeys are almost all intensively reared nowadays. 'Fresh farm' simply means that the bird is fresh, not frozen, and that it comes from a farm. But most farms have now lost the farm-yard image and most poultry is reared in battery units. Driving out into the country in search of a 'real' farm may be reaching for the moon, unless one is very lucky. Much of the poultry sold is deep-frozen for purposes of hygiene and keeping quality, in the circumstances of mass distribution.

When shopping the cost-conscious consumer is looking for food value for money along with good flavour and appearance. As an overall guide, per pound of lean meat, turkey is a little cheaper than chicken, and duck is always a good deal more expensive (about 75 per cent more). The ratio of bone to flesh is always about half and half, and the $2\frac{1}{2}$–4 lb ($1 \cdot 3$–$1 \cdot 8$ kg) birds often work out the cheapest, depending on how the price per pound is structured for different sizes. In large shops the choice of bird will also be between: fresh chilled, either in bags or not, and frozen, either whole or in joints.

Frozen chicken or turkey has to be lower in price to work out cheaper than fresh, cooked weight for cooked weight, as there is always some water which comes out on defrosting and the de-frosted bird is then lighter. Ready-stuffed or pre-basted chickens are sold at the same price per pound as ordinary chickens; in some cases the amount of stuffing used is proportionally great compared with the original weight of the bird. Stuffings are much cheaper than meat, so one can be paying a very high price.

Less-expensive Meats

Much general information is always available through the media
on the use of cheaper cuts of meat. I intend here simply to look at
minced beef, liver, beefburgers and sausages. With these meats it
is important to know something about how the food value may
vary. With other less-expensive cuts the main thing is to make
sure that they really are a good buy in terms of the amount of
lean meat one gets.

Minced beef is a good buy if the quality of the mince is good.
The best mince may have 30 per cent more protein than the
worst, in which the proportion of fat will be a lot higher. Fat
tends to run out of the meat during cooking, so buying a better-
quality mince could be an economy. Another good policy is to
choose a piece of meat and then ask for it to be minced. In the
latter case, though, it is not unusual for a little of the meat to be
left behind in the mincer, and the butcher is not obliged to make
it up to the original weight. Mince should contain no preservatives, except during the summer in Scotland where it is permitted.

Beefburgers and hamburgers all contain beef. The accepted
standard is that they should be composed of meat with cereal and
that there should be at least 80 per cent meat. Sometimes there is
as much as 90 per cent meat, of which 25 per cent may be fat.
Obviously the more fat there is the more shrinkage on cooking
and the smaller the beefburger when served. 'Beefburgers with
onion' sound as though they are providing something extra good,
but these burgers could contain as little as 70 per cent meat.
Minceburgers may contain only 50 per cent meat—that is the
lower limit.

For protein value homemade hamburgers or dishes made with
fresh minced beef are much better value for money, but most
people appreciate the convenience of quick-frozen beefburgers
for occasional use. The other benefit of making burgers from
fresh mince is that they will be additive-free. Some butchers
prepare very good ones too.

Liver is a meat with good protein and excellent iron value. It is
a concentrated source of a number of B vitamins. The fat and

calorie values are fairly low, which is helpful. Therefore many people like to include it in menus once a week, but not more often because of the high cholesterol content. The price compares very favourably with the other less-expensive meats we are considering in this section. Another advantage is that it can be cooked in a matter of minutes, particularly if French recipes are chosen; then it qualifies as a convenience food.

Sausages come midway between minced beef and frozen beef-burgers in terms of food value for money. For protein value mince is 25 per cent cheaper than sausages; you need to eat 8 oz (225 g) sausages to get as much protein as you would with 4 oz (115 g) mince. Sausages are made with meat, cereal (in the form of rusk, bread or rice), water, seasoning, a thin skin and emulsifying salts. Sometimes milk powder or soya bean flour is added to give extra food value, or herbs and spices for extra flavour. The Sausage and Other Meat Product Regulations, 1967, state that the composition of sausages must be as follows:

Type of sausages	*Amount of meat*
Pork sausages	At least 65%
Beef sausages	At least 50%
Pork and beef	At least 50%

Sausages often do have more meat than this but it is useful to know what their minimum food value could be. The homemade alternative to sausages is pork patties, made from a mixture of lean and fat pork with breadcrumbs, egg, salt, pepper and herbs. This way you know exactly what they contain.

Sausage skins may be natural casings made from the gut of pig, sheep or ox, but in commercial sausage-making synthetic casings are used. Sausage skins or casings come like ladies stockings—they can be 'standard stretch' or 'low stretch', in which case they are likely to be made of cellulose. Alternatively—and these are mainly used for cooked sausages like luncheon sausages—they can be no-stretch with a fibrous texture. This type of casing is also used on rolled boned bacon, gammon, ham and brisket, all of which are sliced by machine. Apparently such casings take print very well, so the manufacturer can place his name right on the skin!

The ability of casings to take up colour is made use of in that ace of manufactured foods, the skinless Frankfurter. A special cellulose casing is coated inside with red or orange dye; the casing is then filled with sausage meat and the sausages are dried, during which process the dye is transferred from the inside of the casing to the outside of the sausage. After processing the skin is removed to reveal a delicious skinless Frankfurter tinted orange or red. Needless to say this is not a cheap process.

Neither is the process of making skinless sausages. Skinless sausages do start off with skins, but they are carefully treated by immersing in hot water for a short period so that the surface of the meat becomes firm and the skins can be removed before packaging. This is why skinless sausages cost more than their more common relatives. They do, however, have the edge over other sausages in that they are uniform in length and diameter and cannot easily be squashed, which makes them easier to package. The amenable skinless sausage is obviously the pride and joy of some food technologists!

Dairy Produce

Milk

Milk leads the list of foods with a good distribution of many nutrients. Nevertheless, it is not the perfect food. (This is only true of breast milk as a food for young infants.) Cow's milk is low in iron and some of the B vitamins, but it is a valuable food and should be included in everyone's meal plans. Many different kinds of milk are available:

Pasteurized milk is heated to 162°F (72°C) for about a quarter of a minute, then immediately cooled to 50°F (10°C). This is designed to kill off any harmful germs. All our ordinary silver-topped, gold-topped and homogenized milk is pasteurized.

Silver-topped bottles contain ordinary pasteurized milk with 3 per cent fat.

Gold-topped bottles contain Channel Island milk with at least 4 per cent fat.

Homogenized milk has been mechanically forced through a very narrow channel and on emerging impacted on to a solid plate which causes the fat particles in the cream to be divided into particles small enough to remain suspended throughout the milk. This never separates out again in the bottle, so there is no 'top of the milk'.

Sterilized milk has been heat-treated to 212°F (100°C) for one hour or 250°F (122°C) for fifteen minutes. The heating affects the flavour, although many people brought up in areas where it is the normal milk like it.

Long-life or UHT milk is whole milk which has been ultra-heat-treated to 275–302°F (135–150°C) for only one to three seconds, then packed into sterile cartons. It keeps well for several months; the carton is date-stamped. It costs more than ordinary milk and should be regarded as a convenience food. It has the nutritional value of sterilized milk, without the slightly 'cooked' flavour.

Skimmed milk has had the fat almost completely removed by removing the cream. Consequently the protein content is higher and the calorie value lower (about half that of whole milk). The calcium value is still good, but the vitamin D content is lower because this vitamin is more concentrated in the creamy (fat) part of the milk.

Evaporated milk is produced by vaporizing off part of the water content of the milk, by heating in a vacuum chamber at reduced pressures (this makes water, or milk, boil at low temperatures, and the steam can be removed in this evaporating process).

Dried skimmed milk is spray-dried. A fine spray of liquid milk is introduced into an enclosed chamber in the presence of a stream of hot air. The fine droplets dry immediately and fall to the bottom of the vessel as powder. The food value when reconstituted according to the manufacturer's instructions is the same as that of skimmed milk. There are no additives in dried skimmed milk.

Dried skimmed milk with added vegetable fat. In this product the fat removed by the skimming process has been replaced by vegetable fat. To ensure proper keeping properties, flow properties and satisfactory flavour, specific ingredients and additives are used. Vitamins A and D are also added to replace those removed with the fat. The end result is a very useful and acceptable product in terms of taste, keeping quality and cost. The vegetable fats in these products are not necessarily high in unsaturated fats, however. It is not therefore comparable with the 'filled milks' that were used in the experiments mentioned in the chapter on fats.

My own policy on milk is to take fresh milk from the milkman each day. In my area it is unfortunately not possible to buy skimmed milk, so I use dried skimmed milk powder for cooking in order to reduce our total consumption of whole milk and the 'hidden' fat it contains. And I always have skimmed milk powder with added vegetable fat to make up as 'real milk' if we run short during a weekend. This gets us away from the need to over-order and perhaps therefore over-consume.

Cream is a delicious 'extra' if you like it and if it suits your eating plan to include a little sometimes. The warning sound comes when we see the very high fat content:

Clotted 55% fat	Single 18% fat
Double 48% fat	Half-cream 12% fat
Sterilized 23% fat	

The fat is of course saturated fat, and bad for the arteries unless one is (possibly) well protected against atherosclerosis by having been a brown-bread consumer all one's life.

I feel that cream is a very artificial food, especially when added to an otherwise high-fat diet. In the country situation most of the cream would have been taken for butter-making, leaving the skimmed milk for drinking, at least by the adults. In our home we copy this method in part by using the top of the milk (and silver-topped at that!) to substitute for cream where possible. For special-occasion desserts I use the thinnest cream which will whip (i.e. a mixture of double and single). I whip this up and pipe into rosettes, which can be frozen and then used one or two per serving when needed. Being mean with cream is in my opinion being cruel to be kind!

Yoghurt in its plain form has been eaten for hundreds of years in warm countries, especially the Middle East. It probably originated as curd cheeses did, as a way of preserving milk produced in excess of immediate requirements. It has always been associated with healthy diets.

Unfortunately very soon after plain yoghurt arrived on the British market, manufacturers discovered that the public preferred sweet, colourful yoghurts—no wonder when the British are so addicted to 'nice puddings'. Now special yoghurts have come to dominate the market to such an extent that they are now often cheaper than plain yoghurt.

Real fruit yoghurts top the sales, the favourites being blackcurrant, strawberry and raspberry, followed by bilberry, blackberry, pineapple, apricot, mandarin and orange. The turbidity and solids of the yoghurts may make the fruit or juice appear pale in colour and weak in taste, so artificial flavours and colourings are often added to reinforce the effect of natural fruits. In fact the flavouring preparations often contain a large proportion of fruit essences. In some countries only genuine fruit and fruit essences are permitted and no colouring. It is important to read the labels; some yoghurts will contain real fruit and others just fruit flavourings. Carton size varies, too, and price is no guide.

The alternative is to make your own yoghurt. This will cost about a quarter as much as prepared yoghurt in terms of ingredients. A yoghurt-maker set may be used, or simply an insulated container. Chopped fruit can be added quite successfully provided that both fruit and yoghurt are well chilled before combining.

EGGS
Eggs are one of the cheapest foods for animal protein; one egg can give us 10 per cent of our total protein requirement per day plus 10 per cent of our iron. It is an easily digested food and also supplies vitamins A, D, B_1 and riboflavin. However, the food value can be wasted; for example, overcooking of fried eggs renders them indigestible. Hens are very efficient producers of human food; a 1 lb (0·45 kg) hen may produce 250 eggs per year, that is 4 lb (1·8 kg) protein, 3 lb (1·35 kg) fat and 3 lb (1·35 kg) calcium carbonate (shell).

When purchasing eggs, consumers think about size, price and freshness. As we have already seen, small or medium eggs (sizes 5 or 6) work out cheaper than sizes 3 or 4 if they are more than 5p less per dozen. And white eggs are better value than brown because they are usually cheaper but have the same nutritional value.

Freshness of eggs is sometimes a problem. A farm will have the freshest eggs of all, and after that the best choice is to buy from one of the quality-conscious supermarkets. Eggs from small stores and from the milkman may be less fresh; one has to assess quality on a trial basis.

Labelling of egg boxes conforms to EEC regulations. This is how the code works:

> The first number means country of origin.
> The second number means region.
> The third number shows when packed, i.e. the week of the year.
> The extra number shows the actual date of laying.

The week number refers to the week of the year, numbered 1 to 52. The discerning shopper needs to have a week-numbered calendar. This will enable you to get as far as discovering which week the eggs were packed, but the extra information about the specific day of laying is not often available. One needs to bear in mind that the packers usually only call once a week at each farm, so the egg could be seven days old when collected and up to two weeks old when labelled. Some supermarkets stamp the actual day of packing, which is helpful. It is possible for eggs to be labelled as packed three weeks ago, yet really to be five weeks old.

Fresh farm eggs, grade A, should pass this test: broken in the pan they should look like this in cross-section:

Cross-section of an Egg

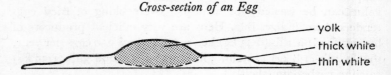

yolk

thick white

thin white

If they are not fresh the thick white will have turned into thin white, which then runs flat over the pan, losing the compact shape. They are not harmful in this state, but neither are they the quality one has paid for.

CHEESE

This has been called the King of Foods. It has good food value and versatility in food preparation, and a great range of flavours and textures are available. It is made in summer from surplus milk in milk-producing areas, so the map of cheese-producing areas is the map of some of our best farmlands.

A general rule about the food value of cheese is that the harder in type the cheese, the more protein it contains, and this means in practical terms Cheddar cheeses and Edam. Weight for weight, cheese has more than one and a half times as much protein as roast beef or cod, and it is of course much cheaper. Cheese protein is rather short of one amino acid, but fortunately one that is present in good quantities in bread, so bread and cheese are very good together as a protein food combination.

If one is concerned about weight then cottage cheese will give less calories because the fat has been removed. Conversely, cream cheeses give more calories because they are made from cream rather than from whole milk, and the fat content is higher. The best keeping quality is found in Cheddar and Cheshire cheeses. A Cheddar which the family really likes is therefore the best choice.

Buying for a cheese board often involves choosing from small, ready-cut, wrapped portions of different shapes and sizes. The price per pound is always stated.

A family cheese board based on English cheeses is the best choice from an economy point of view; even Stilton, our most expensive cheese, costs considerably less than some of the French cheeses, delicious though they are.

Storage is important for all kinds of cheese. Normally you want to arrest the maturing processes which change the flavour and so you should store cheese at 50°F (10°C) or below, i.e. in a cool larder or the refrigerator. But it is important to allow the cheese to come to room temperature for a couple of hours before serving, in order to enjoy the flavour fully. The best wrapping for cheese is aluminium foil, pressed tightly against the surfaces. Polythene film is the second choice, but this must be loosely wrapped to prevent condensation forming on the surface.

Cottage cheese is a fragile product, delicately flavoured and depending heavily on refrigeration for keeping. It is a modern product and not at all like the original cottagers' cheese (which does keep well). Cottage cheese was developed in the USA and involves a process of treating skimmed milk with an acid to coagulate the protein, then washing the curd to produce the characteristic cottage cheese curds. It is very useful in slimming diets as it combines well with numerous vegetables and fruits and has only a quarter of the calorie value of Cheddar.

Cream cheese at its best is a delicious cheese for a special meal but because of the high fat content it should be used in modest amounts. Its quality depends on that of the cream which has been used. There has in the past been a tendency for some people to think that any kind of cream is good enough for cheese, so it pays to choose a reliable make and to buy from a shop which stores it in a carefully run refrigerator.

Bread and Flour

Modern methods of milling flour facilitate very accurate control of how the wheat grain is split, and it is possible to remove or retain any part of it. Thus the millers can provide housewives and bakers with very great variety:

Wholemeal flour, for those who like to keep to wholegrain foods as much as possible.

Wheatmeal flour, 80–90 per cent extraction, for those who want a brown loaf with a better 'rise'. This will have only two-thirds as much fibre as wholemeal flour and its use is perhaps best suited to making pastry or cakes where brown flour is preferred.

Strong white flour, used for making white bread and rolls. To prepare this flour for both commercial and home baking hard wheat must be imported from a country such as Canada.

Soft white flour, made from English soft wheat. It makes cakes rise well and is used in the preparation of biscuits to give a short texture.

Self-raising flour, for convenience in home baking for those who do not want the complication of measuring out raising agents (like bicarbonate of soda and cream of tartar) to add to the flour.

Wheatgerm flour, which contains the endosperm and wheatgerm but no bran. The bread made from it has good food value but a lower fibre content than wholemeal products. This flour is only available commercially.

Granary flour, wheatmeal which has malted grains of barley and rye added to give extra flavour and a nutty quality.

Although white flour has the bran and wheatgerm removed, it has its nutritional value restored to a large extent by the addition of iron, vitamin B_1, nicotinic acid or nicotinamide (another vitamin) and chalk (known as creta preparata). The relevant Food and Drugs regulation states that these additions must be made to all flours except for wholemeal flour, where 'such nutrients shall be naturally present and not added'. The addition of chalk to white bread was introduced during the 1939–45 war in order to improve the calcium content of the nation's food at a time of food restrictions. It was also decided that all breads should be made up to the vitamin B and iron standards of wholemeal bread.

Other additives are anti-staling agents which enable bakers to make loaves that will keep well for up to two weeks, and flour improvers. The latter are added because freshly milled flour does not make good bread, and an improver has the same effect as storing flour for a period of time.

The best white bread is made from strong flour that comes from hard wheat grown in Canada. In dough-making this flour takes up a lot of water, giving a big volume of loaf per pound of flour. This gives light-textured bread which many consumers enjoy and it is a profitable line for the baker. Wholemeal bread has too many granular particles to give a high-rise, light-textured load, but if the flour is from a good wheat the end result will be delicious.

Until very recently white bread has always been a status symbol. For example in Roman times flour was sifted to obtain white flour for the nobles, wholemeal flour being considered good enough only for ordinary citizens. Slaves, convicts and prisoners were required to make do with the roughest flours plus the siftings. This pattern has been followed all through the ages but nowadays the reverse is true; wholemeal bread is becoming a food for the discerning, as the dissatisfaction that some people feel about white bread has turned them to look for something more interesting. In favour of white bread it must be said that it is a standard, reliable product which keeps well, and its nutritive value has been safeguarded by enrichment (with minerals and vitamins). Nevertheless, medical opinion is now beginning to favour brown bread. Probably the strongest reason for this is the recent publicity about the value of cereal fibre and the knowledge that wholemeal bread contains three times as much fibre as white bread does. Wheatmeal loaves come between the two.

Biscuits

Commercial biscuit-making is a large-scale copy of home baking, but manufacturers are able to buy special low-protein (very soft) flours which make their products shorter and crisper. A proteolytic enzyme or sulphur dioxide may be used to soften the flour further, preventing any trace of toughness in the final product.

The nutritional value varies from one type of biscuit to another. Obviously wholewheat or digestive biscuits, which are not very sweet, are a good choice. The best-sellers, however, are always the chocolate-coated ones, followed by the cream-filled varieties. One should consider these as occasional treats rather than everyday fare.

Cakes

Again home baking is emulated, but on a commercial scale special high-ratio flour can be used. This means flour which is able to take up large quantities of fat and sugar. It is interesting to note that a good recipe for a cake made commercially twenty-five years ago contained only half the fat and eggs that are considered 'right' today. Less baking powder is needed now because more eggs give a better rise, but the disadvantage is that more fat and eggs may not be good for people's total fat and egg intake. It depends how much and how often cake is eaten.

Breakfast Cereals

All breakfast cereals contain a fair amount of starch, i.e. carbohydrate, and some protein, but not a large amount. However, as cereals are always eaten with milk, a bowl of cereal may give a child or an adult one-eighth of his daily requirement of protein, plus some vitamins and minerals. If the cereal is brown, the fibre content will be helpful too. On the other hand, it may give an adult one-tenth of his calories for the day, and if he is overweight, and partial to a cooked breakfast, can he really afford this?

The original cereal of this country was, of course, porridge, made from oatmeal. I wonder how many people nowadays even know how long traditional porridge takes to make. I don't mean the instant kind or porridge made by the more laborious three-minute method. I mean real porridge. Traditionally, oats had to be soaked overnight, and then cooked for a few minutes in the morning, or otherwise cooked for between half an hour and an hour in the morning. Today's 'quick' porridge oats avoid the need for all this.

Of course they are more expensive because when we buy a packed of rolled porridge oats, or any other breakfast cereal, we are buying maid service. The same is true of many present-day convenience foods. In the case of other breakfast cereals we are paying for very complex and sophisticated manufacturing processes. How much we pay will depend on the complexity of the process, how many extras are added, what other people like, and how well the marketing of the particular cereal is going.

Breakfast cereals have become extremely important in households where the mother has an outside job. Breakfast may be a rush with everyone eating at different times, so considerable time and effort are saved by children pouring a meal into a dish from a cereal packet and a milk bottle. How wise it would be, though, to upgrade such meals by choosing wholegrain cereals, adding some wheatgerm and fruit, fresh or dried, and going very easy on the sugar. Best of all is to buy a muesli base (flaked wheat, rye and barley) and add wheatgerm, fruit and nuts.

Today's ready-to-serve cereals are made mainly from maize, wheat or rice and can be bought puffed, flaked, shredded or formed into granules. For some extra cost they can be supplied ready-coated with sugar, honey or malt—a bit more maid service. Some will have extra vitamins and minerals added too.

A simple wheat or rice grain destined for the *puffed cereal* packet leads a most exciting life. First it is skinned by a wet scouring process, then it is sealed into a puffing gun, a pressurized steam chamber. Suddenly the pressure is released and the wheat grain and its thousands of companions each swell to several times their size. Finally, it has to be toasted. While all this is going on it is being advertised, marketed and generally made into a more expensive product than simple unprocessed wheat or rice. The same applies to other ready-to-serve breakfast cereals, each processed in a different complex way.

Fresh Fruit and Vegetables
Fresh fruit and vegetables are expensive items on the shopping list, but not more so than cakes, biscuits and pre-prepared puddings. It is a good idea to choose consciously from a list of vitamin C-rich produce, remembering also to choose carrots and/or tomatoes frequently for vitamin A. Remember too that it is good to eat at least half or this food raw.

Vitamin C Value in January, February and March

January

Potatoes	Oranges
Cabbage	Seville oranges
Broccoli	Grapefruit
	Bramley apples

February and March

Potatoes	Oranges
Cabbage, Savoy and spring	Grapefruit
greens	Pineapple
Broccoli	Bramley apples
Green peppers	
Tomatoes	
Watercress (March)	

Recipes

Baked jacket potatoes:
> Served with butter and black pepper
> Stuffed with grated cheese, chopped hard-boiled egg and
> bacon, chopped chicken, ham or prawns

Cabbage salad:
> With grated carrot and onion
> With celery, apples and raisins
> With peanuts or cashew nuts and lemon
> With pineapple and/or green pepper
> As hot cabbage salad, made by cooking shredded in-
> gredients lightly in oil, then adding a little vinegar before
> serving

Cabbage:
> Selected in variety. There are January Kings, Savoys, Drum-
> heads and red cabbage. Cook in a minimum of water for the
> minimum of time and add chopped onion, very thinly
> sliced carrots or apples, or herbs, to give interesting flavours

Green peppers:
> Stuffed with rice, raisins and herbs, Greek style
> Stuffed with tuna fish and rice
> Stuffed with chopped tomatoes, grated cheese, parsley,
> lemon juice and yoghurt, served cold
> Some good Chinese dishes use green peppers with pork or
> chicken

(*see over*)

Bramley apples:

> Apple sauce, which is served in Holland with numerous dishes, while we tend to restrict it to pork meals
>
> By this time of the year Bramleys are sweet enough to use raw, and make a good salad with celery, cheese and dates
>
> For a colourful pudding stuff the centres of Bramleys with a few cranberries before baking

Oranges:

> Sliced with lettuce while tomatoes are expensive
>
> Combined with mustard and cress (grown on the window-sill) while lettuces are expensive
>
> Use Seville oranges in any recipe normally using lemons

VITAMIN C VALUE IN APRIL, MAY AND JUNE

April

New potatoes
Cauliflower
Greens
Spinach
Purple sprouting broccoli
Radishes
Watercress

Citrus fruit from Israel
(This is the time to use frozen or canned fruit as fresh fruit is expensive during April and early May)

May

New potatoes
Broccoli
Cauliflower
Green peppers
Spinach
Tomatoes
Radishes

Fruit, as in April

June

Potatoes (very plentiful)
English tomatoes
Radishes

Cherries
Raspberries
Strawberries

June

Peppers
Green peas
Primo cabbage
Broccoli
Spinach

Recipes

Cauliflower main dishes:
> Cauliflower cheese
> Cauliflower milanaise
> Cauliflower polonaise
> Cauliflower, carrot and lentil curry
> Stuffed cauliflower, centre scooped out and filled with chopped cauliflower, tomato, onion, chopped peanuts and hard-boiled egg
> Cauliflower and apple salad

Spinach:
> With eggs
> Spinach omelette with grated cheese topping, flashed under grill
> Spinach quiche
> As filling for pasta
> As a salad

New potatoes:
> As a dish in their own right. Simply wash off the earth, cook for the minimum time in salted water, and serve with butter and chives. Alternatively serve with a fondue of tomatoes and onions gently cooked together

Other suggestions:
> Cheese and tomato fondue
> Stuffed tomatoes
> Peas bonne femme
> Potato salads
> New potato mould

VITAMIN C VALUE IN JULY, AUGUST AND SEPTEMBER

July

Vegetables as June	Blackcurrants
Turnips	Raspberries
	Strawberries

August

Vegetables as June	Blackcurrants
French beans	Redcurrants
	Loganberries
	Strawberries

September

Runner beans	Cooking apples
Broccoli	Blackberries
Peppers, red and green	
Red cabbage	
Spinach	
Tomatoes	

Recipes

Tomatoes (now at their best):
    Stuffed with tuna or eggs
    Cooked with courgettes
    Grilled with herbs, to accompany meat

Other suggestions:
    Green bean and pepper salad
    Green bean, bacon and egg salad
    Peperonata
    Ratatouille
    Freezer jams with no cooking
    Summer holidays are a good time to eat as much raw food as
    possible. Look for recipes using young turnips in light sauces,
    e.g. lemon sauce

Vitamin C Value in October, November and December

October

Brussels sprouts	Apples
Peppers	Pears
Spinach	
Tomatoes	
Turnips	

November

Savoy cabbage	Cooking apples
Broccoli	Cranberries
Brussels sprouts	Mandarins
Red cabbage	Tangerines

December

Broccoli	Cooking apples
Brussels sprouts	Cranberries
Green peppers	Mandarins
Red cabbage	Satsumas
Tomatoes	

Recipes

Brussels sprouts:
> With chestnuts as a main dish
> With leeks
> As salad
> Puréed

Red cabbage:
> Made into sauerkraut
> Braised with chestnuts

Other suggestions:
> Spinach salads with bacon, nuts or tomatoes
> Jacket potatoes with butter and chopped sage, topped with
> apple slices and returned to oven for 20 minutes to blend
> the flavours

Recipes may be found in: *Summer Cooking*, Elizabeth David, Penguin; *Health Food Cookery*, Marguerite Patten, Hamlyn; *Fresh All the Year*, Gail Duff, Pan.

'Quick-frozen' Food

Quick-freezing is the most natural way of preserving food because freezing is a reversible process. Provided that both the freezing and the thawing are done carefully and correctly the food virtually returns to its original condition in colour, flavour and texture. Then provided that the end cooking is carried out according to the instructions given for each particular item, the nutritive value of frozen food is going to be high. In the case of vegetables the time between harvesting and freezing is very short compared with the 'transport-plus-selling' time for fresh produce, and this is a great advantage in retaining the vitamin C value. The freezing process in effect 'stops the biological clock', preventing the action of enzymes causing over-ripeness and the activity of micro-organism causing spoilage. Quick-freezing produces results closely resembling the best unpreserved examples of a very wide range of foods. It is especially successful with vegetables, fish, meat and many types of cooked food.

Another virtue is that compared with competing methods of food preservation, such as canning, freezing uses least energy overall, even including the energy needed in the cold chain (that is depots, shops and homes) after manufacturing.

It is worth looking at a few products in detail to get an idea of how foods are prepared and frozen. The ones I have chosen to 'profile' are frozen peas, frozen fish fillets and the very successful Chinese dishes produced by one major firm.

Peas for quick-freezing are likely to be grown by English farmers under contract to the frozen-food company. This helps to ensure that the factory eventually supplies just what the customer requires. Farmers who own land close to the factories agree to grow special seed supplied by the company. The farmer works closely with the company's fieldsman and plants his seed when he is given the go-ahead. The growing crop is watched carefully by both men, and they jointly consider all crop treatments such as fertilizers and weed-killers.

When the crop is approaching maturity, the fieldsman gives the farmer the word to begin harvesting. This is carefully timed so that the crop can be delivered to the factory in perfect condition and at just the right time to fit into the factory's production schedule, which has to cope with similar crops from many other farms in the same area. Thus the farmer's fields have become the first stage of factory production. The advantage to the farmer is that he knows well in advance that his market is secure and he receives payment at the time of harvesting. For the consumer, contract farming means that a uniform standard of quality is established and held.

In the factory, peas are quick-frozen by the air-blasting method. In the most modern development they are borne along a tunnel by a cushion of freezing air forced up from below. This keeps them separate, so that they can be easily and separately packed into polythene 'handipack' bags. The process takes only a few minutes, after which the food is transferred to a low temperature cold store where it is kept at $-20°F$ ($-29°C$) until it is needed for distribution. As a seasonal vegetable, which the food manufacturers make available all the year round, some peas must of course be stored for up to twelve months.

Fish fillets are processed at factories built specially near the trawler ports. In the factory the fish is washed, filleted and skinned if necessary. Then it is packed into flat cartons and subjected to plate freezing. The cartons are placed between narrow metal shelves in which a very cold refrigerant circulates, freezing the packed food by contact with the cartons. Like the peas the fish is then held in cold store at $-20°F$ ($-29°C$) and at this temperature it could be kept without spoiling for many years.

The Chinese food which has been so successfully produced and marketed by one major frozen-foods manufacturer is an excellent example of a convenience food designed to make unusual and exotic cooking easy for us. It is so easy in fact that in our home an older child can take charge of the meal. The range of Chinese foods was developed at a time when the success of Chinese 'takeaways' was very obvious. With the frozen products we are offered a meal of very high quality and complete freshness.

It is interesting to note that the products were developed with the help of a good Chinese chef. There was also help from consumers who took part in research projects concerning their preferences in Chinese food and their reactions to what was being produced at the pilot-scheme stages. The firm had many problems to overcome regarding ingredients, supply and technology, as Chinese cooking is so very different from ours. Not least was the problem of obtaining really fresh beansprouts, which Chinese restaurants tend to grow on the spot. Making new foods commercially is a hazardous business, requiring great expertise in research, raw-material buying, processing, quality control and marketing. In the case of these Chinese foods it has been a very worthwhile venture.

WHAT CAN I AFFORD?

Decisions about how much money to spend on food are a highly personal matter. Some people keep to a comparatively low figure, but the cost of eating out in a restaurant once a week may be half as much again as their total food bill for the week. Others spread small pleasures over the whole week, preferring to enjoy many 'evenings in' rather than a single 'evening out'. One elderly lady recently commented that, as her age had lowered her food requirements and the rise in prices had lowered her spending power, she now gives herself just one meal a day, but an extremely nice one! The principle is the same but her particular plan could not be recommended for health reasons.

Frugality works best where there is mutual agreement about the need for it and where some other benefits of it are visible. For example, cutting the everyday food budget may make it easier to afford to entertain or to consider supporting a child in the Third World.

How Can I Economize?

We need to think about food costing and buying good nutritional value for our money. One simple way of doing this is to consider foods in the following groups:

A. Milk, cheese, eggs
B. Meat, poultry, fish
C. Dried peas, beans, lentils, nuts
D. Bread, rice, pasta, oatmeal (for porridge or muesli), flour (for home baking)
E. Ready-made breakfast cereals, cakes, biscuits
F. Vegetables
G. Fruit

The cost of one's food will depend on how much comes from each group. For example, if you decide to make your meals mainly from meat, poultry, fish and fresh fruit and vegetables (groups B, F and G) your costs will be high. If, on the other hand, you halve the number of times group B foods appear on your weekly menu you will lower your costs. You can then substitute with some of the following:

DISHES COMBINING GROUPS:

A, D and F: Pies or savoury flans and quiches with a variety of fillings based on vegetables, eggs and cheese.
A and D: Flour plus milk and eggs for pancakes.
A, D and G: Batter puddings with fruit.
A, D and F: Vegetables with cheese sauce served gratinée. Vegetables with milk to make soups. Bread to accompany.
C and F: Pulses and vegetables for main-course soups.
C, D and F: Vegetable and bean risottos. Dahl, lentil curry with rice.
A, F and G: Salads with eggs, cheese and fruit added.

Substituting D for E means being prepared to do more home mixing and baking, but there are easy dishes to make with whole grains. Most wholemeal or oat-based cakes, puddings and biscuits are undemanding of skill compared with the intricacies of sponge-cake making. An added advantage is that homemade wholewheat cakes and biscuits keep better. They also last longer because they are more satisfying as foods and tend to be eaten in smaller quantities.

The other possibility is to use small quantities of foods from group B combined with other foods, as described in the chapter on protein. You can feed four people on a bean casserole for the same cost as giving two people a casserole of stewing steak.

How much you spend depends, of course, on how much meat and what quality you choose. Some people spend far less than others on food simply because they have not become used to eating very large portions of meat or fish—or several unnecessary protein courses in a row. Many people would prefer to enjoy meat in small portions rather than be deprived of it. The convenience factor of grilling or roasting a good cut of meat also has to be considered. Cheaper dishes are usually more labour-intensive, but a collection of 'easy' ones is well worth making.

GROWING FOOD AT HOME, THE CHEAPEST PATH TO CHOOSE

Growing food at home is an excellent idea provided you have knowledge, space, time and energy.

Knowledge can be painlessly acquired by following one of the television series and purchasing the accompanying handbook. The combination of expert advice, actually seeing things done at the right time of the year, and a well-illustrated book to refer to, gives you an excellent start.

Space may be limited but these schemes are designed for small plots, perhaps only 10 feet by 12 feet (3 by 3½ metres). If you have more space then a book like *Grow Your Own Fruit and Vegetables*, by Laurence D. Hills (Faber, 1973) will be helpful. Alternatively you can simply scale up the plans in the television books.

If you want to be completely self-supporting and grow all your own fruit and vegetables you may need to rent an allotment. Allotments are rented from your local authority, which is obliged to provide them if application is made by six registered electors or ratepayers.

Many people do not want to get as involved as this and decide to specialize in a few crops, such as runner beans and lettuces, or tomato plants grown by a warm wall. There are even schemes for mixing up flowers, fruit and vegetables, growing Morning Glory flowers over the runner beans and courgettes in the azalea bed.

Time and energy are often at a premium but one gardening scheme works on the basis of just two hours' work a week right through the year. Obviously this is sometimes heavy work such as digging or harvesting potatoes. At other times it will be quite light: planting out, hoeing, tying up plants. Watch a professional gardener at work and see how he paces what he does. He spends quite a lot of time leaning on his spade just looking at the garden, not because he's lazy, but because short bouts of heavy work interspersed with rests enable him to keep going all day. Many amateur gardeners work flat out for an hour or so and wonder why they feel so exhausted or damage their backs. Hardly surprising when this energetic activity contrasts so sharply with their sedendary weekday work.

Perhaps the most important thing of all is that the person who is going to provide the muscle power behind the vegetable-growing scheme is the one who is really committed to the idea in the first place. Willing slaves become less willing as watering every evening in June is followed by hoeing in the hot sun in July and digging up potatoes in August!

The advantages of home growing are that it saves money and that really fresh salads and green vegetables are available exactly when required. You also have the option of growing produce without chemical pesticides or fertilizers and there is considerable satisfaction in the work.

The disadvantages are that the main summer growing season is short so that one has to be an expert on timing, and watering has to be well organized at all times. Seeds, compost and fertilizers are increasingly expensive, but there are many ways of cutting costs. For example, I have grown crops quite well using three-year-old seed. It is soon obvious whether they are going to germinate or not.

Returns for your money. For lettuce, if one costs up seed, peat pots, compost and slug pellets, it has been reckoned that you would spend about £2 and get a return of £25-worth of lettuce in a season, using cloches for part of the time.

For runner beans, if canes have to be bought as well as seed, liquid fertilizer, peat pots and compost, in the first year you will only do a little better than buying beans. However, bearing in mind that canes last at least five years, the cost can be spread. Then the return is about three times the initial outlay if you would normally purchase fresh beans and nine times your outlay if you would normally buy frozen beans throughout the year. Choosing highly recommended varieties is well worth considering to ensure a good return for your efforts.

Herbs are a very easy addition to the garden. They virtually grow themselves once they are established. They are then available for winter drying and add flavour to countless dishes.

11. Balanced Diet, Flexible Meals

The classic joke about a balanced diet is that it means heavy first courses followed by light puddings, or vice versa. This might sometimes be a guide to not consuming too many calories, but it is easy to think of any number of high-calorie light puddings to ruin the argument and one's figure at the same time! *A balanced diet* is one which contains all the ingredients that a particular individual needs for health and energy (see Part One of this book).

FLEXIBLE MEALS

With the pressures and variety of lifestyles arising in modern life meals must be flexible. I like to think of this flexibility in terms of *flexi-time* and *flexi-food*.

Flexi-time is a concept with which most working people are familiar. Staff choose their own working hours, thereby getting less crowded journeys, long lunchtimes or time off for hairdos. Flexi-time with regard to meals has been a housewife's problem for a long time; the jokes about the dried-up meal waiting in the oven are not at all funny when that meal was shopped for and cooked with love.

Useful recipe books have been written to help solve this problem, and they are well worth consulting, as some foods can easily be kept hot, whereas others spoil easily in terms of flavour and food value. My own experience has been built up during several years of having to run a school taxi service in the three-quarters of an hour immediately before 6.45 p.m. supper on weekdays.

Add to this the fact that one member of the family comes home at variable times, and everyone arrives home needing to eat as soon as possible, and you have a problem. The following ideas have been helpful.

Casseroles or salads are the best choice in these circumstances. Homemade soups can be made into a major part of the meal. One simply looks out for soups that are a cross between a soup and a stew, namely those that contain some meat or fish, lentils, beans or peas. Add dumplings or good bread and, if you are still worried about the protein content, grated cheese to sprinkle on top. As some members of the family won't bother about the cheese, while others will take more than is good for them, small side plates of grated cheese can be organized on an individual basis. To keep the soup hot there is nothing better than a wide-necked thermos flask, particularly when some people are going to be late.

An individual attitude to serving food makes flexible timing easier for the one who is catering. Individual side salad bowls can be prepared, and each person adds his own salad dressing when he is ready to eat. Dessert prepared in individual dishes is far more attractive, as the last person coming to a large dish may find just the unattractive remains of what was originally a very nice-looking pie. Jacket potatoes 'stagger' very well. Small ones cook faster and can be served to children before the parents eat. If the father is really late, jacket potatoes keep hot perfectly. Very good cakes and pies are the most flexible dessert, apart from fruit and fruit salads.

A well-prepared 'cook-it-yourself' course is often quite acceptable. For an individual, cooking something easy can be relaxing and enjoyable. For example:

> A hamburger or two in rolls to eat with the prepared salad bowl
>
> An omelette with a choice of fillings, again pre-prepared
>
> Pancakes (good for demonstrating culinary skill of the most showy kind!)

Continuing the self-service theme, you could provide small

dishes of yoghurt with a choice of toppings to add: hot apricot purée (Greek fashion), chopped nuts, grated chocolate or sliced banana in lemon juice. A do-it-yourself 'icecream parlour' is a special treat. The important thing about encouraging self-help is that if the meal has to be served to different people over a period of two hours, the cook does begin to feel like a worker in an all-night café, cooking one egg here and heating up a bowl of soup there in a very inefficient way. Planning ahead to prevent this is a great help.

Flexi-food means having a plan for group eating that enables everyone to have basically the same food, but because individual needs vary there are items on the menu which will automatically allow for variation. For example, a family might sit down to the following meal:

Bean and bacon hot-pot
Watercress and cucumber salad in individual bowls
Jacket potatoes with butter
Apples, cheese, wholemeal bread
To drink: wine, milk or water

The father takes something of everything, but avoids the butter (because he doesn't need it and is better without it) and just eats the jacket potato along with the hot-pot. He takes a glass of wine or water, as he does not need to drink milk in quantity. His milk was taken in the morning with his breakfast cereal and in various drinks during the day. The teenage boy takes two jacket potatoes with his portion of hot-pot. He drinks a glass of milk and enjoys bread and cheese as a second course. He has had plenty of protein, calories, calcium, iron and vitamins. He has forgotten the apple, but is advised to take it away to eat later in the evening. His teenage sister has one small jacket potato with the casserole, has to be encouraged to have a glass of milk and rounds the meal off by eating the cheese and apple without bread. This is because she is calorie-conscious. Her mother's choice is similar, but having had a teatime snack she is less hungry than the others, so she misses out the jacket potato and takes a little wholemeal bread to eat at the same time as the casserole. The apple alone is sufficient to finish with, but she will enjoy some milky coffee after the meal.

This is 'flexi-food'; portions and choice can be varied to suit individual needs.

HOW MANY MEALS A DAY?

People have been shown to be healthier and absent from work less often if they have frequent meals. A pattern based on five meals a day, with elevenses and afternoon teas including protective foods such as milk, fruit, tomato or egg and cress sandwiches, is good, particularly for people whose three main meals are spread over a very long day. When the in-between meals are nothing but sweet drinks and buns or biscuits they are neither satisfying in terms of keeping up our energy and concentration levels, nor good for teeth and possible weight problems.

It has also been shown that eating small meals more frequently is less likely to cause overweight than eating just one or two large meals. This is because moderate meals provide the energy needed for consumption in the next few hours without excess, which might cause us to store up the spare calories as fat.

If you eat five meals a day, three of these meals might each give a quarter of your daily requirements of nutrients, while the two snacks might each give an eighth. Alternatively, you could eat three meals a day, each giving one-third of your daily requirements.

THE IMPORTANCE OF BREAKFAST

Studies have shown that those who eat breakfast have more energy and better powers of concentration during the day than those who skip it or choose their food poorly at this time of day. One important point is that the meal should contain some protein, and that this protein should be of good quality. Then there will be a slow release of the nutrients during the course of the morning. If, on the other hand, the meal consists of a cup of sweet coffee or tea with very little milk, plus quickly digested starch and sugar in the form of white toast and marmalade, the blood sugar level will be quickly raised soon after the meal, providing immediate energy but keeping very little for the second part of the morning. It has even been shown experimentally that whatever sort of lunch people eat, a good breakfast actually enhances their energy and concentration levels during the afternoon as well.

Breakfast should be thought of as one of the main meals of the day, and as such we should make sure that it provides one-third of our daily food requirements.

Fruit is the best appetizer. During the week fruit juice is the simplest choice as an appetizer and to supply vitamin C. This may replace early morning tea or be taken as a first course. Fresh grapefruit can be used at the weekend because there is more time, and it makes breakfast more of an occasion. Remember that just half a small orange or one-quarter of a small grapefruit provides half the daily requirement of vitamin C (see p. 105).

Some energy food is needed. This is likely to be taken in the form of porridge, cereals or bread, carbohydrate foods which contain their own built-in vitamin B_1 for energy. Several spoonfuls of sugar stirred into a cup of coffee may have the same energy value, but because it lacks vitamins the sugar would not be helpful nutritionally. The bread and breakfast cereals will of course give you some protein and iron as well. If they are wholemeal products the fibre will be right too. Also, they will be digested more slowly and the nutrients released over a period of time.

Some protein should form the main part of the meal. This is important both for the growth and repair of body tissues and also to make the breakfast last through the morning.

Adults can happily take their breakfast protein from cereals taken with milk (the best choice would be muesli or porridge), or from wholemeal bread along with a milky drink of coffee or chocolate. For children it is better to include some protein of animal origin, and the most usual and cheapest food selected is an egg. Boiled or poached eggs are the easiest to digest.

Above all, things have to be easy in the morning, easy to pre-

F

pare and easy to wash up. Good equipment helps, and I would put an egg poacher and one or two non-stick pans way above an automatic toaster when choosing breakfast-making equipment.

Variety in the Breakfast Main Course—What You Gain and What it Costs

An egg. A standard egg, size 3 or 4, weighs about 2 oz (60 g) and supplies about an eighth of an adult's daily requirement of protein and a tenth of the iron requirement.

Bacon. One slice weighs about 2 oz (60 g) and gives half the protein of an egg and half the iron. It is good for extra vitamin B, but costs at least twice as much as an egg.

White fish. A 3 oz (90 g) portion gives twice the protein and three-quarters of the iron provided by an egg. The cost is about three times that of an egg.

Kippers. A 3 oz (90 g) portion would again give twice the protein in an egg, about two-thirds of the iron and cost three or four times as much.

Kidneys—making breakfast in the grand manner. A 2 oz (60 g) kidney gives one and a half times the protein of an egg and four times as much iron and costs three or four times as much.

It is a good idea to have breaks from cooking. Foods suitable for a cold breakfast are ham, tomatoes and soused herrings. The Dutch make good breakfasts with thinly sliced cheese.

It has been said that 'one man's breakfast is another man's lunch or supper', and certainly the principles discussed here could be applied to other meals during the day.

AN INEXPENSIVE BALANCED DIET

A balanced diet need not be an expensive one. Indeed, thinking rationally about food choice can result in a trimming of the budget—and the figure too. A very inexpensive balanced diet was designed by some Canadian nutritionists, seeking to find the best low-cost meal plan. This is how a typical day worked out:

Breakfast:	Porridge with wheatgerm and raisins.
	Toast, margarine and molasses (which provides iron and other trace elements as well as sweetening).
	Chocolate-flavoured milk.
	(I should also like to include a vitamin C fruit.)
Lunch:	Indian lentil soup.
	Open sandwiches of peanut butter served with turnip sticks.
	Sliced oranges.
Snack:	Crunchy whole oat and nut cereal with raisins, eaten as 'nibbles'.
	A hot fresh lemon drink, slice of lemon on top.
Dinner:	Minestrone soup.
	Spaghetti with tomato sauce and a sprinkling of grated cheese.
	Coleslaw—cabbage plus sliced green pepper, radish and celery with a dressing.
	Apple crisp—sliced apples baked with crunchy oat topping.

The regular shopping list for their eating plan included:

Grains

Wholewheat flour
Rolled oats
Brown rice
Dark rye flour
Pearl barley
Millet
Peanuts
Other nuts and grains

Animal protein

Eggs
Skimmed milk powder

Pulses

Split peas
Soya beans
Other beans or lentils

Vegetables
Cabbage
Carrots
Potatoes
Turnips

Fats
Fortified margarine
Vegetable cooking oil

Sugars in limited amounts
Honey
Molasses
Brown Barbados sugar
Raisins
Dates

Extras sometimes purchased
A little cheese
Good herbs
A few special fruits and vegetables according to the budget
Meat and fresh milk, bacon occasionally

It would take too long to discuss the values of this way of eating, but it may help to consider that it is:

—Inexpensive.
—Healthy.
—Ecologically sound.
—Convenient, in that shopping for many of the major items need only be done occasionally.
—Delicious, if you use a little ingenuity.

CAN A SNACK LUNCH REALLY SUBSTITUTE FOR A COOKED MEAL?

There is no particular merit in hot food, except that it is comforting on a cold day. It is also helpful for older people, but others will gain as much energy and warmth from a well-chosen snack.

The chart (p. 167) shows how comparable snacks and hot meals can be. For protein the snack wins over the hot meal because of the protein value of bread. The snack is higher in fat,

COMPARISON OF THE NUTRITIONAL VALUE OF A SNACK AND A COOKED MEAL

	Weight		Energy	Protein	Fat	Carbo-hydrate	Calcium	Iron	Vitamin B_1	Vitamin C	Vitamin D
	oz	g	kcal	g	g	g	mg	mg	mg	mg	mg
Snack meal											
Bread, wholemeal	4	115	272	10·8	3·6	52·8	32	3·6	0·28	0	0
Butter	0·5	15	104	0·1	11·5	0	2	0	0	0	0·18
Cold roast beef	2·5	75	160	13	12	0	5	1·25	0·05	0	0
Tomato	1	30	3	0·2	0	0·7	4	0·1	0·02	6	0
Lettuce	0·5	15	1	0·2	0	0·2	3	0·2	0·01	2	0
Apple	4	115	52	0·4	0	13·6	4	0·4	0·04	4	0
Milk in coffee	2	60	38	1·8	2·2	2·8	68	0	0·02	0	0·02
Total			**630**	**26·5**	**29·3**	**70·1**	**118**	**5·55**	**0·42**	**12**	**0·20**
Cooked meal											
Beef, roast	2·5	75	160	13	12	0	5	1·25	0·05	0	0
Cabbage, boiled	2	60	10	1·6	0	1·4	22	0·2	0·01	12	0
Potatoes, roast	6	170	192	4·8	1·8	46·2	18	1·8	0·18	12–42	0
Peaches, canned	4	115	100	0·4	0	26	4	2	0	4	0
Custard	3	90	78	2·7	3	11·1	93	0	0·06	0	0·03
Total			**540**	**22·5**	**16·8**	**84·7**	**142**	**5·25**	**0·30**	**28–58**	**0·03**

F*

however, but this could be moderated by spreading the butter thinly and removing visible fat from the beef. Each meal makes a reasonable contribution to the daily requirement of calcium. For iron the value is the same, nearly half an average daily requirement. If the snack consists of cheese sandwiches the iron value would be lower and the vitamin D value higher, but it is sensible to compare meals based on the same protein food. With cheese sandwiches the meal would still provide a third of the day's iron. Notice that the vitamin C content is higher in the cooked meal, but the range given for the cooked food depends on different summer and winter values in potatoes. Also poor cooking could lower these values. 12 mg vitamin C from the snack meal is a very acceptable contribution to the daily requirement—about 30 mg. The energy values are given only in calories as this adequately demonstrates that both meals supply sufficient energy food.

BALANCED AND FLEXIBLE PACKED MEALS

A general strategy based on the following formula is a recipe for success.

—Wholemeal bread for carbohydrate, protein and fibre as well as some iron and B vitamins.
—Margarine or butter for fat, but not too much.
—Cheese, eggs or fish for protein, vitamins and minerals.
—Raw vegetables and fresh fruit for vitamins C and A and more fibre.
—A drink, which should be milk for children and might be fruit juice for adults.

This may be presented either as sandwiches, taking the raw vegetables as finger food, or as salads including the cheese, eggs or fish (packed into a sealed container to be eaten with a fork). This latter course is very helpful for people who have low energy requirements, i.e. women, men with sedentary jobs and anyone who has a weight problem, because the amount of bread can be reduced or they can eat crispbread. It is a particularly good way of providing a flexible picnic for a family because everyone can eat the right amount of the main protein irrespective of how much bread they choose to eat. Even a strict weight-watcher can join in.

Below is a selection of packed lunches to show how these ideas can be applied:

—Double-decker sandwiches of wholemeal bread, one layer filled with sardine or tuna fish, one with chopped hard-boiled egg
Raw carrot sticks
An orange
Homemade cake or biscuit (using nutritious ingredients), for those with high energy requirements
Milk to drink for children

—Wholemeal sandwiches filled with cottage cheese and walnuts, or cottage cheese and crisp grilled bacon
A hard-boiled egg
A tomato
A banana or, for those with high energy requirements, a slice of fruit pie
Milk as above

—Homemade bacon and egg pie or quiche
Tomato or watercress and celery
Wholemeal bread and butter plus cheese, or crispbread and cheese for those who need less food
An apple
Milk as above

—Chicken joint wrapped in foil or grated cheese or tuna fish packed in small container
A salad with any of the following: shredded cabbage, grated carrot, cucumber cut into chunks, chopped celery and

green pepper, tomatoes, spring onions, radishes. (If the meal is based on chicken the joint should be prepared so that it can be eaten as finger food, taking a fork for the salad. The cheese or tuna fish can be packed in a separate container and added to the salad at the meal time.)

Bread and butter sandwich or crispbread

A pear, or a wedge of pie for the extra hungry

Milk as above

BALANCED FOOD AT A BARBECUE

Barbecues can be an excuse for overeating, particularly as they are associated with hospitality and entertaining. Meat, often in large portions, is the main feature of the meal, with lavish basting increasing the fat content. The cheaper alternatives of sausages and hamburgers also make a high-fat meal. If barbecuing is a regular method of cooking it is worth noting that charred meat may be a source of carcinogens, so some foods should be cooked in foil rather than on the open grill.

How can barbecues be made into balanced meals? This is such an enjoyable way of eating that it is worth giving a little thought to making it nutritious too.

Cooking poultry or fish is a good idea. Chicken quarters take about forty minutes to cook through on the grill, turkey drumsticks need one and a half to two hours. Fish you will need to wrap in foil or skewer on a spit, as cooked fish is easily broken. Timing varies according to the size of the fish, and a meat thermometer is very useful for testing (internal temperature of cooked fish should be 140–45°F (60–63°C)).

To balance the meal, items which can be cooked on the grill are: onions, green peppers, mushrooms, tomatoes, corn-on-the-cob, small parboiled potatoes.

Further additions to the meal which enhance the food value are: salads in variety, including rice or pasta salads and hot garlic- or herb-flavoured bread or rolls.

For an interesting main dish try Keftalia, which are homemade sausages. Combine finely-minced lean beef and lamb in equal proportions, then add chopped onion, parsley, tomato flesh, mixed spices, salt and pepper. After mixing well shape the sausages ready for cooking; nothing is needed to bind the mixture. These are good nutritionally and delicious too.

BALANCE WHEN SIX 'SPECIAL' DIETS COME TO SUPPER

A number of people are put on to diets for medical reasons, usually because some part of the body is not functioning normally. In their own home eating sensibly is straightforward, but we can help to make social occasions easier for them by suiting the menu to the guest and providing treats which will cause no embarrassment. Most people will tell you what their restrictions are, although some not wishing to make a fuss will say nothing. In these circumstances it is useful to have a rough idea of what might suit them.

The following are general ideas for what might be easy and acceptable, but in each case there may be some other factors involved. The idea is to help you to plan the occasional meal for visitors; should you be providing for a longer period of time you will need much more detailed advice.

For a diabetic the timing of meals is usually important, so keep to the time that you have said the meal will be. The diabetic's diet is likely to include control of the amount of carbohydrate eaten, and sometimes the amount of fat is significant too. To make the meal easy to enjoy:

Avoid: Fried food (grill instead).
Soups, stews, casseroles, sauces and gravies which have been thickened with flour.
Stuffings.

Provide: A roast or grilled main dish or a casserole in which the gravy is thickened with egg or tomato-purée.
Plenty of low-calorie vegetables (see pp. 88–9).

A fruit bowl to substitute for forbidden puddings and cakes.
Starch-reduced rolls or crispbread.

A weight-watcher will be happy to be catered for in the same way. You could entertain them on the same evening!

After a gastric ulcer plain, soft food is needed. The specific diet varies from one patient to another, but these guidelines may help:

Avoid: Meat soups, stocks and gravies which stimulate the flow of gastric juices.
Highly flavoured foods and fried foods.
Very hot or very cold food.

Provide: Grilled or poached white fish.
Boiled ham.
Plain roast chicken.
Creamed potatoes, mashed carrots, asparagus tips, marrow or ripe raw tomatoes with skin and pips removed.
Milk pudding, yoghurt, baked custard with baked apple, ripe bananas, peaches, pears.

Gall bladder trouble generally calls for meals containing much less fat than usual.

Provide: Homemade vegetable soups, plus Melba toast.
Very lean meats, baked, boiled or grilled.
Plainly cooked vegetables, keeping to the milder flavoured ones. A really delicious platter of a variety of vegetables would be most welcome as this is a very dull diet.
A milk pudding or custard made with skimmed milk, fresh or stewed fruit, low-fat cheeses.

For a low-protein diet, sometimes needed for adults with kidney complaints:

Provide: Very small portions of meat, fish, eggs and milk.
Bread and cereals may be restricted too.
Vegetables, except for peas, dried beans, baked
beans, broad beans and lentils, all of which have a
high protein content.
Fruits of all types, prepared in any way.

Don't be surprised if the visitor takes only vegetables or salad
with some bread, bypassing the main dish. The fruit course will
be especially important to such a guest, so go to town on making
it very attractive.

For a sufferer from gout, which is due to a fault in metabolism, in many cases inherited:

Provide: Vegetable soup, grapefruit or melon as a starter.
A main course based on eggs and/or cheese, for
example a quiche or soufflé.
Fruit of any kind.

There are many other conditions requiring dietary care. I have
chosen some of the more common ones, which I have personally
encountered amongst friends and acquaintances. Many people
will agree that in an age in which the pleasures of the table are
greatly valued it is an asset to know how to provide the right kind
of hospitality for everyone, including those who either temporarily
or permanently are not blessed with cast-iron constitutions.

BALANCED MEALS WITH NO COOKING

Even those who love cooking also enjoy a holiday from it, and
some of us like small holidays quite often! One of mine comes on
Sunday evenings when I set out on wooden platters and wooden
bowls a selection of cold foods based on what is left at the end of
the weekend. Cheese, nuts, pâté sometimes, sliced salad vegetables, brown bread, butter, a fruit bowl and perhaps some homemade biscuits can make an impressive buffet if you concentrate

on an artistic 'still life' type of layout. It takes only five or ten minutes to prepare. From then on it is self-service, and each member of the family is free to choose the combination of foods they most enjoy. One makes up a salad plate, one likes really beautiful open sandwiches. A third who is always hungry specializes in 'Scooby snacks', triple-decker sandwiches bursting at the seams. The 'must have something hot' addict makes cheese on toast with a sprinkling of herbs and some tomato slices to simulate pizza.

When we visited Verulamium, the excavated Roman town at St Albans, an exhibit which particularly interested us was the simple Roman meal. There was our Sunday supper: brown bread, cheese, fruit, nuts and a glass of wine. We should have been quite happy to join them!

A 'pub lunch at home' means to us two kinds of bread and three kinds of cheese, celery, tomatoes and homemade pickle, plus something nice to drink with it—in our case lager or apple juice. Sometimes there will be a slice of pie or flan to follow, homemade and kept in portions in the freezer. Such a meal can be an 'occasion'. Eaten at a small table set by the window on a sunny day, there is all the difference in the world between this and the 'only bread and cheese' attitude.

For a more elaborate lunch at home, but only taking a few minutes for two people to prepare together, we use large flat plates and arrange items in a wheel shape:

> Grated carrots and nuts (sliced together with a shredding machine)
> Celery, date and apple salad
> Canned sweetcorn
> Tomatoes, cucumber and peppers in French dressing
> Sardines, tuna or grated cheese

Another way not to cook so much is to 'think big' every time you do have to slave over a hot stove. Decide to cook more than you need for a particular meal. You can then cool the remainder rapidly and keep it in the fridge for a couple of days ready to present in a slightly different form on a second occasion. The important thing is to actually divide the soup, casserole or pudding into two parts immediately after cooking so that the cooling can be really effective. It also prevents the 'third helpings brigade' from spoiling your lovely plan, otherwise the effort will have been in vain.

THE FOOD VALUE WE 'COOK AWAY'

Whilst 'spring cleaning' our recipe collections in terms of food choice we can also look for ways of improving cooking methods, possibly even changing recipes slightly to preserve and enhance their food value.

Vitamin C in vegetables and fruits is well worth conserving. It is no use selecting vegetables for their high vitamin C content and then losing much of it during the preparation of meals. We have already discussed storing, preparing and cooking vegetables to retain vitamin C (see pp. 107–8).

Recipes in which such foods as tomatoes and potatoes are cooked for longish periods of time, as in soups, casseroles and sauces, could in many cases be adapted so that these important ingredients are added at a later stage than usual. Tomatoes can be puréed or liquidized, then added very near to the end of the cooking time. If they are needed to give flavour to the dish some concentrated tomato purée can be added at an earlier stage, saving the fresh tomatoes for addition just before serving. Similarly, add chopped watercress or parsley to a soup during the last few minutes before ladling out, to give maximum vitamin C value. A good minestrone soup recipe starts with the ingredients that need the longest cooking, beans and onions, then come the carrots, followed by the macaroni, shredded cabbage five minutes before the end of the cooking time and chopped tomatoes last of all.

Turning to fruits, in some puddings it is possible to add orange slices or orange and lemon juices at a quite late stage in the cooking process. 'No cook' freezer jams, in which fruit purée is mixed with sugar and pectin, preserve the food value of the fruit as well as the delicious summer flavour.

B vitamins and fibre can be important features of homemade breads, cakes, pastries and puddings. If the ingredients list includes wholemeal flour, oatmeal, nuts and dried fruits (for natural sweetness) it is possible to bake with less sugar. Thus there is a higher vitamin and fibre content, for the amount of calories provided, than there are in baked goods containing a lot of refined flour and sugar. As far as raising agents are concerned, baking powder has the effect of destroying some of the B vitamins, whereas yeast actually adds more.

Protein in all foods of animal origin benefits us most if it is gently cooked. It then becomes soft and easily digestible. Cheese should never be overcooked, as the protein shrinks and toughens visibly. If milk is boiled and the skin is removed from the surface some valuable protein will have been sacrificed. Lightly cooked eggs, soft-boiled or poached in water containing no salt, provide the most easily digestible protein. To add extra protein to mashed potatoes, dissolve skimmed milk powder in some of the potato water and use instead of adding cold milk. At the same time some of the vitamins and minerals are being added back from the potato water.

As one begins to think in terms of food value one gradually collects extra ideas for making the most of the good foods selected. Many of these also serve to improve the flavour and appearance of the final dish, so that the medical-sounding 'balanced diet' finally becomes a culinary delight.

12. Liquid Refreshment in the Jungle

In 1976 the total expenditure on food purchased in the UK was estimated at £14,180 million, of which £1,000 million was spent on non-alcoholic drinks. To this £1,000 million add the expenditure on alcoholic drinks, which was £5,980 million, and we can see that as a nation we spend half as much on 'liquid refreshment' of one kind and another as we spend on food. This chapter aims to give some insights into what is in the bottles, cans and jars we so much like to buy.

WATER

Water is not strictly speaking a food because it does not directly enable us to grow or produce energy, neither does it provide us with protective factors. Nevertheless, our bodies are made of 50–65 per cent water, the exact amount depending upon our age and how fat or thin we are. In this water are dissolved all the chemical compounds that go to make up our complex cells and tissues. All the body's chemical metabolic processes take place in watery solutions. For this reason water is ultimately more important than food, and shortage of water causes more immediate and more intolerable distress than shortage of food. In cases of starvation people can survive much longer without food than without water.

Our bodies are constantly losing water as we eliminate waste products from the bladder and the bowel and as we perspire and respire (breathe), and yet the water content of each individual remains amazingly constant. Most people would be surprised to know that about one-third to one-half their water intake comes from the water present in solid foods. The other half to two-thirds must be taken as fluids, and a 'thirst mechanism' organizes us to drink enough to cover our needs.

In a temperate climate we need to drink at least 2 pints (1·2 litres) of fluid each day. Factors which increase our needs for fluids are:

a. Doing heavy work.
b. A rise in climatic temperature.
c. A meal containing a lot of protein.

People changing from a fibre-depleted diet to a full-fibre diet also need to be sure to drink sufficient water. Bran, for example, has the quality of absorbing quite a lot of water, thereby fulfilling its function of adding bulk to our food.

Water with meals is a sensible choice for every day. It is not desirable to take it just before a meal, however, as it then tends to dilute the gastric juices which are waiting to start the processes of digestion. Water also partly fills the stomach, and this fact is utilized when slimmers are asked to drink a glass of warm water before meals to reduce the appetite. It is best to drink water late in the meal or afterwards, when it does not dilute the meal, but rather forms channels through the food and passes independently through the stomach to be absorbed in the large intestine.

We enjoy choosing our favourite drinks, but what the body needs is the water from these drinks. The body would be just as happy with cool, fresh, plain water as it is with tea, coffee, wine and fruit squash—in fact it might be happier. We give our bodies a lot of extra chemical sorting out to cope with as we provide ourselves with great variety in liquid refreshment. Let us look at some of the most usual drinks, starting with tea and coffee.

TEA

Tea is a pleasant drink, especially if different varieties are tried. It has been said that a passion for tea is a notorious British national characteristic. This may have been reinforced during the thirteen years between 1957 and 1970 when the retail price of tea did not change. Thereafter prices began to rise, and it has been forecast that we may have to wait until 1985 for tea to be cheap again. Tea and coffee prices are linked as they are considered alternative drinks; where one is in short supply or highly priced there will be a greater demand for the other. Both depend on climate. Frosts and cyclones can suddenly alter predicted crops.

Tea gives us small quantities of caffeine and tannin, greater amounts if it is brewed for a long time. It is surprising that a strong cup of tea contains as much caffeine as an average cup of coffee. Both caffeine and tannin are stimulants, and some people seem to be mildly addicted to them. For most people this is a harmless thing, but some have been cured of feeling 'ill' by removing tea and coffee from their menus. An alternative is to use herb teas.

Teabags have been used in the USA since the 1920s and in this country in more recent years. These prevent over-brewing because the strength of the brew in terms of caffeine and tannin content, as well as flavour, can be more easily controlled by removing the teabags from the pot at exactly the right moment. Teabags cost 50 per cent more than packeted tea, but they are much more convenient. Note that brands with perforated bags may brew no more quickly than plain ones, and beware of new bigger bags until you are sure that they contain more tea than the little old ones.

Herb teas. Some of the herbs which make really pleasant drinks are lemon thyme, mint, parsley and peppermint. All these can be grown at home very cheaply and easily, even in a window-box. The method of making tea from fresh herbs is to 'bruise' the leaves of a small bunch of herbs, then use them to make an infusion in boiling water exactly as you would with ordinary tea. Herbs can be dried for use in winter or purchased from health-food stores.

COFFEE

Coffee is expensive. The trees which produce the coffee bean are slow to mature and need careful husbandry; the crops are vulnerable to the weather and there is the further cost of long distance transport. It has been suggested that both tea and coffee should be considered luxuries and imbibed with care and appreciation.

Coffee with chicory. Adding chicory has been a way of lowering the cost of coffee whilst retaining a good flavour. Chicory is the root of wild endive and it is dried, partly caramelized and ground, then added to coffee in varying proportions. The attraction is its cheapness.

Decaffinated coffee is used for people with heart conditions for whom caffeine has an adverse effect. Caffeine can also have an over-stimulating effect on the bladder, and it excites the nervous system, making people more wide awake, tense and irritable. Headaches and palpitations can be side effects.

Instant coffees are available in three main types:

1. Spray-dried instant coffee was the first to be invented, liquid coffee being sprayed through hot air to produce a powder.
2. Freeze-dried instant coffee is produced by freezing a solution of coffee, then reheating in a vacuum.
3. Spray-dried granular instant coffee involves the amalgamation of grains of spray-dried coffee into larger particles.

Freeze-dried coffees tend to have more caffeine than the spray-dried kind; they also produce a flavour nearer to that of ground coffee. They are usually the more expensive of the two. Refill packs cut costs, or catering sizes may be purchased. With a large pack it is always worth repacking into smaller sealed units to conserve the flavour.

Coffee whiteners have become popular as substitutes for milk, particularly at work. It is convenient to have milk or cream substitutes readily available and hygienically stored where no refrigeration is available. Coffee whiteners are sophisticated products, whether they are packed in glass jars for general use or produced as 'one-cup packages'. They are very artificial foods being made from glucose solids and vegetable fats, but they are pleasant, convenient and only used in small quantities anyway. If added to several cups of coffee each day the calorie value might be too high, and in that case skimmed milk powder would be a better choice.

COCOA

Cocoa has traditionally been the school child's bedtime drink. It is a good source of iron and with the milk makes a good contribution to the diet. It is necessary though to boil cocoa with the milk and this 'inconvenience' has undoubtedly led to the popularity of drinking chocolate as a substitute. This is a truly instant food, popular also because it is ready-sweetened. Like all chocolate products it contains cocoa as the main ingredient.

Some people are allergic to cocoa. This has been discovered particularly in some migraine sufferers, where banning cocoa and chocolate from the diet has effected a marked improvement.

Carob powder, which provides a chocolate-like taste, is the alternative to cocoa. It is obtainable at health-food stores, and often suits those who cannot take cocoa. It is easy to digest due to the low fat content, and furthermore it does not contain any tyranine, an amino acid in cocoa which causes migraine for some people.

Carob powder can also be successfully used in cooking. Like drinking chocolate it can be whisked up in milk using a fork and no cooking is needed.

VEGETABLE JUICES

Generally only tomato or mixed vegetable juices are available ready made, but anyone with a juice extractor, separator or liquidizer will find 'juicing' a good way of using surplus garden

produce at times of glut. However, it must be realized that
drinking the juice is the lazy way of eating the vegetable. There
is real merit in chewing raw vegetables. Also if the juice is
strained during preparation much of the fibre is wasted. So do
not make juice-drinking a substitute for salad-eating.

FRUIT JUICES

Fruit juices are excellent as food when taken in reasonable quantities. Their value for vitamin C has already been discussed (see
p. 106).

Long fruit drinks taste nicest when made from fresh fruits and
juices, but sadly many children brought up on fizzy drinks and
highly flavoured and coloured squashes will find them rather
plain and not sweet enough. It is worth persevering to get
homemade drinks accepted.

MANUFACTURED SOFT DRINKS

What do manufactured soft drinks contain? One particular
advertisement offered us 'all the glory of the protopectinoids and
the bioflavinoids'. This made it sound very special but in fact just
indicated that the drink contained plenty of the skin and pith of
the oranges along with the juice. Generally no one tells us what
exactly is in soft drinks, except in low-calorie products, but there
are regulations about the making of all fruit drinks and squashes.
If you know the basic facts the name of the type of drink tells you
a lot:

A squash or cordial will contain 25 per cent fruit juice in the
bottle before you dilute it.

A crush is a ready-to-drink squash and must have at least 5 per
cent fruit juice.

A fruit barley water must have 15 per cent fruit juice before
diluting.

A fruit drink is made with at least 10 lb (4½ kg) whole fruit per gallon (4·5 litres), includes the flesh and peel pulped, and is therefore about 50 per cent fruit.

All these drinks must have a minimum amount of sugar, which is equivalent to one heaped teaspoon per glass when it is made up, and the amount of saccharin that can be added is controlled.

A fruit-ade or fruit-flavoured drink implies very little or no fruit. These -ades are mostly fizzy drinks.

All the drinks mentioned may contain permitted amounts of flavouring, colouring and preservatives.

Cola drinks are made with flavourings of sugar and saccharin and added phosphoric acid which counteracts the excess sweetness. They have nothing to recommend them nutritionally. Indeed, there is concern that the combined sweet and acid effects may be very bad for children's teeth. Most colas also contain caffeine, one can of cola being equivalent to a small cup of coffee. One or two brands are made specifically without caffeine, and if children insist on having colas these are the ones to choose.

ALCOHOLIC DRINKS

More than half as much money is spent on alcoholic drinks as is spent on food each year in the UK. The nutritional value apart from calories tends to be low, but the value of some drinks as relaxants, appetizers and therefore as aids to digestion must be mentioned.

The characteristics of alcoholic drinks most likely to interest people are the flavour and appearance, the price, the alcohol content and the calorie value. The flavour and appearance can be left to the expert wine tasters and the price to the retailers; for the purposes of this book a few nutritional facts and figures follow.

Alcohol content and calorific values are listed in the tables overleaf. Regarding alcohol content you will see that beer looks innocent, but these are percentage values and don't forget that beer is always served in large glasses.

Alcohol Content

Drink	Alcohol content
Beers	3–5%
Wines	10–12%
Sherry/port	18–20%
Spirits	57–70%

Calorific Values

Drink	Measure	kcal	kJ
Beer	½ pt (300 ml)	90	377
Strong ale	½ pt (300 ml)	170	712
Cider	½ pt (300 ml)	87–235	363–982
Sherry	1½ fl oz (45 ml)	55–65	230–272
Red wines	1 wine glass	62–72	259–301
White wines	1 wine glass	74–93	309–388
Gin	1½ fl oz (45 ml)	105	438
Whisky	1½ fl oz (45 ml)	120	501
Vodka	1½ fl oz (45 ml)	150	627

Sparkling grape and apple juices, which are unfermented, are a very good alternative to wine. They give a sense of occasion to many family meals and are a treat which children can share. They cost less than wine, and getting out the best glasses makes all the difference.

13. The Future Jungle

This final chapter is about the trends and counter-trends which may influence the way the Food Choice Jungle looks in the future. Will the Jungle become denser or will there be fewer new products? Will the increase in leisure hours result in a swing back to the use of simple basic foods, because there is more time for cooking? After all, convenience foods have boomed during years of full employment and the forty-hour week. Their raison d'être may be gradually removed by the growth of automation in industry and the consequent lessening of time pressure on individuals.

We have today a fast-rising world population, people are changing their lifestyles both in developed and underdeveloped countries, and there are international agreements and disagreements about trade in foodstuffs. Bad harvests in one country may seriously affect the staple food supply of another. In this situation the incentives for a nation to produce as much of its own food as possible are great. On a smaller scale, too, there is a desire on the part of individual families to pursue the 'good life' of self-sufficiency. But the major changes we are likely to see in the future are linked closely with availability.

AVAILABILITY OF FOOD IN THE FUTURE

Two major factors have always played a very large part in deciding what people ate, namely availability and price (which partly reflects availability). In the West the most serious problem of availability are likely to be concerned with the provision of animal protein at reasonable prices, especially meat and fish.

Fish—Where Will it Come from?

Fish is seen by nutritionists as a valuable animal protein food. The protein value is good, fish is easy to digest, and whatever fat there is will be of the unsaturated kind. It has been described as our last major *hunted* food. As such it carries with it unpredictability of location, physical danger for the hunters, and disputes about territorial rights. One of the most interesting questions is how much we will see fish *farmed* in the future? This may be a key factor affecting availability, and may come about in two ways:

1. *Sea lochs* in an area like Scotland could be enclosed so that salt-water fish could be reared in a controlled and protected environment. As breeding and the rate of extraction could be carefully controlled, all young stock could be brought on to the best advantage. In the future this might replace some of our distant-water fishing.
2. *Inland fish farms* have already started to produce several thousand tons of fresh-water fish each year, and we can expect an increase in their number. This is not seen as a substitute for hunting fish but rather as a supplementary industry. Farmed fish are cheap to produce compared with animals because they are cold-blooded and therefore do not use food to keep warm. This means that they are very efficient converters of protein feedstuffs into animal protein: 60 per cent of the protein they are fed turns into 'fish'. Whereas animals have been farmed for centuries, fish farming is a new technology. For successful development the needs are completely reliable water supplies and first-rate stockmanship. As these can be provided, all the signs are that we shall see more fresh-water fish on the market in the future.

Fish may also come from Antarctica in years to come. It has been estimated that the crustacean fish, krill, might be harvested from the waters of the Southern Ocean in quantities almost as great as the total annual harvest of marine fish throughout the world. A number of nations are already fishing krill on an experimental basis, but as krill is a very important part of the ecological chain it will be necessary to come to international agreements about research and development of this food resource.

Fish and the Food Manufacturers

The processing of fish in recent years has demonstrated that food manufacturers can play a great part in enabling us to use what is available. You will no doubt realize, for example, that there are two kinds of fish finger nowadays: cod fish finger and unspecified fish fingers which are generally made from coley (a smaller and less white fish than cod, but with good flavour and texture and much cheaper). This illustrates well the trend towards using less-attractive-looking but good-tasting fish—dabs are another example. At the time of writing an unusual smaller member of the cod family called blue whiting is being harvested experimentally by deep trawling.

The tendency for the future in sea fishing would therefore seem to be to harvest a lot of smaller varieties in addition to the larger ones and to find acceptable ways of preparing them for the table. This will mean the provision of good recipes for using the new types of fresh fish, but as many of these varieties require care, time and trouble in preparation I think we are also likely to see even more quick-frozen, 'fresh from the sea' and 'ready-to-grill' products, where someone else has already dealt with the problem of skins, tails and bones!

More or Less Meat?

The expense of converting vegetable food into animal protein in farming has already led to high meat prices, encouraging people to accept the introduction of meat extenders in the form of tex-turized vegetable proteins. Perhaps we can also hope for a swing towards the intelligent use of unprocessed vegetable proteins, together with more information about their balanced use. Our way of eating would be enhanced if we learned to use beans, lentils and nuts, as suggested in Chapter 4.

Of course it would be possible to carry factory farming further than we have done already, so that the whole process of food production would be designed in purely chemical terms. This is what might happen:

Dark, tinted water containing the appropriate chemicals could be exposed to artificially focused sunlight from which it would collect energy. The water could then be fed into tanks and used for growing microscopic plants at great speed under high pressure. Some of this plant material could, with added vitamins and minerals, be fed direct to animals to provide real meat for special occasions. Some of it could be made into flour and oils, and some could be processed into butter and cheese. The protein in much of the plant material could be extracted and spun into texturized vegetable protein. In time quite realistic 'fillet steaks' might be on the market.

I think this is unlikely to happen. I think that sheep will continue to graze and that cattle will continue to be reared in conventional farm conditions because our country is well suited to them. However, there are signs that they will become increasingly expensive creatures to nurture as the cost of feedstuffs increases. This is likely to happen as less-developed countries begin to make better domestic use of the crops which we now import from them relatively cheaply. They may also acquire Western tastes and increase their consumption of animal protein. We would then find imported feedstuffs even more expensive, and our meat consumption would tend to decline. In the past the West has emphasized animal protein and the Third World has struggled to exist on vegetable protein. In the future there may be more balanced consumption of both types of protein everywhere.

Much research has been done on the extraction and use of leaf protein for human consumption. It is possible for this to be eaten as a supplement to other proteins, and its use has significance particularly in rainy countries where crops do not ripen well. A more detailed discussion of this subject is beyond the terms of reference of this book.

Making the Best Use of What is Available

If the availability of key foods for the future is in doubt, making the best use of what is available will become more and more important. Manufacturing methods will undoubtedly reflect problems of availability, so we can expect two major factors to be well to the fore:

1. The reduction of waste in food processing.
2. The conservation and enhancing of the nutritional value of individual items.

Reducing wastage in food processing will probably account for some curious manufacturing processes. We are all accustomed to the idea of small pieces of fish trimmed from fillets being used to make fish cakes, but a similar process is used to turn meat trimmings into something far superior to the original ingredients. By dicing, cooking and shredding oddments of meat and blending them into a paste of raw meat, a food material can be produced capable of being 'reformed'. This means pumping it through a nozzle to produce large slabs, which are then set by heating in a steamer. During this process the fibres can be lined up to look like meat, so that by the time it is cooled and sliced it looks very good. 'Reforming' is also currently used in the preparation of 'snack' foods, usually of the potato chip or crisp variety. Dehydrated potato is reconstituted with the addition of plenty of tempting flavour and colour, then squeezed out of tubes into a variety of shapes ready for frying and packeting. The trend to watch for here is that certain health-conscious food manufacturers have it in mind that it would be a good idea to up-grade such 'snacks' by adding protein, vitamins and minerals.

Preservation of nutritional value, flavour and texture. With every year that passes, these qualities are given greater emphasis in food manufacturing. It has been said that every natural food carries its own micro-nutrients, i.e. the vitamins and minerals which the body needs to make good use of that food. But some processing methods do change the natural balance of nutrients in foods, and manufacturers are now aware of a responsibility to replace any deficits where possible.

One new development in food preservation is the process known as *aseptic canning*, which can be used for liquids and pastes. It is already in use for UHT milk and for dessert puddings, and is likely to be developed for products like canned meats. Food is sterilized in specially designed heat exchangers before filling into sterile cans, whereas normally food is sterilized after canning. This enables manufacturers to make more-nutritious foods with a better flavour and improved keeping quality.

It is also very likely that one of the future trends will be that *less additives* will be allowed in our foods. We have in the past been permitted to add a greater range of non-food ingredients than many other countries, but Common Market regulations will probably bring us more into line.

WHAT OTHER CHANGES ARE WE LIKELY TO SEE IN THE SHOPS?

I'd like to suggest that we should expect most of the following:

More Brown Flour Products and Perhaps 'Instant Brown Rice'

The recent emphasis on the value of wholegrain foods will hopefully result in a demand for more brown flour breads, cakes and biscuits. Items which we could previously only obtain from health-food stores are now appearing in supermarkets. An example is the wholemeal (brown) pasta now widely available. Brown rice is not at present very popular because it takes longer to cook than white rice, but I think we may well expect it to appear on the market in a partially cooked form as 'instant' or 'easy-to-cook' brown rice.

Unfamiliar Fruits and Vegetables

Experts are constantly seeking to breed new varieties which will enable farmers to produce more food per acre, together with strains that resist a variety of weather conditions. It is important, too, to grow varieties which mature at regular intervals, as anything which extends the harvesting season is very helpful. This is particularly so where expensive harvesting equipment can be used over a longer period each year, thus lying idle for less time. New strains of fruits and vegetables are also being developed which better withstand processing by freezing or canning. This has happened with peas, beans, celery and tomatoes, and the research will continue.

One very interesting point is that although scientists are very pleased with the new varieties they are keeping 'seed banks' of the now obsolete varieties to be grown in the future if the new ones should become susceptible to disease. So grandfather's favourite variety for home growing may well make a comeback as just what is needed some time in the twenty-first century.

Fewer Damaged Vegetables and Better Grading of Produce

Mechanical harvesters are being designed so that more and more crops can be gathered automatically. This means that in some cases farmers can plant their rows of crops closer together, thus growing more per acre. Multi-row bean harvesters and pod viners for peas make this possible and harvesters are being produced for crops as small as carrots and pearl onions. But the big problem with mechanical harvesters is that vegetables can easily be damaged, so we shall need the best of machines and very careful grading of produce in the future.

New Convenience Foods

It will be interesting to see how far manufacturers continue to provide us with even more convenience foods. We already have orange juice without having to squeeze oranges, instant porridge, preformed bacon slices, ready-sliced bread, freeze-dried coffee and instant tea. It is possible to grill a pre-prepared portion of meat, fish or chicken, boil your vegetables in a special polythene bag, rehydrate some potato and stir the instant pudding mix into milk. Alternatively, we make a sandwich with slices of cheese and bread from packets, take the lid off a canned fruit pie and pop it into the oven for 30 minutes, during which time some water can be boiled to reconstitute a soup mix. This food is not designed for use on a spacecraft or a mountaineering expedition; this is convenience food for families for everyday use!

Tubes of margarine are on the way if the experience of other countries is anything to go by; they make it possible to add a blob of margarine to vegetables without the trouble of getting a knife out. Hard-boiled eggs are already being produced in long roll shapes, with the yolks of many eggs formed into a long thin cylinder surrounded by a cylinder of egg whites. This is put into the centre of veal and ham pies, making each slice more uniform.

We have become accustomed to 'slimming foods' designed to provide everything one needs for a meal in two biscuits. This is likely to be extended to snack foods, and we shall then be getting quite near to the early space travellers' provisions. Will a budding 'new products' man read this book and then design 'the most nutritious of snacks'—high-fibre biscuits sandwiched together with no-cholesterol, low-fat cheese? That would be a convenience food which made an outstanding contribution to nutrition!

More Labelling on Food Packages

When I go to buy my 'ever-readies' I do not need labels. I know what is in cheese, peanuts, oatmeal, cabbage, carrots and raisins, for example. But if I shop for convenience foods there will be a strong element of the unknown: How much meat is there in the ready-made dish of lasagne? How much cheese? Is there enough protein to share between three or four people? What is the fat content? Is it made with a rich sauce or a comparatively low-calorie one?

We have, in the space of a comparatively few years, reached the stage at which food scientists can change the nature of many foods:

a. Fat can be removed from milk.
b. Saturated and unsaturated fats can be balanced in margarines, and special low-fat margarines are produced.
c. Protein can be added to almost anything.
d. Protein can be removed from flour and cereal products, as in the preparation of dietary foods for medical purposes and in biscuit-making.
e. Vitamins and minerals can be added as required.
f. Carbohydrate is the easiest thing of all to add to a canned or packaged food. The carbohydrate may be sugar or starch. Either adds bulk very cheaply, and any resulting over-sweetness or plainness can be masked by seasoning.
g. Numerous low-carbohydrate and low-calorie foods are prepared for diabetic patients and for slimmers.
h. Fibre can be provided 'solo' as bran, rather than in its natural state, i.e. associated with wholegrain products.

Thus food is manipulated and changed. This has been very useful and even life-saving for people requiring special diets.

Changing the nature of foods for healthy people can be questioned, however. Food processing is a wonderful thing, but the continual need to produce a new line can result in the creation of some bizarre mixtures. Now that we are buying 'products' rather than just 'food', we need to know the detailed nature of each product. In this respect full labelling would be a great help.

Changes in Retailing Methods

Food could be retailed more efficiently and its quality could be improved if all traders had the best possible transport, storage and stock control.

Very large frozen-food-distribution depots placed strategically throughout the country could receive food from manufacturers' cold stores, quickly delivered in bulk and entering the depot through port doors; refrigerated containers could then emerge from a different set of doors to deliver to out-of-town hyper-markets and shopping complexes; in the shops upright-freezer wall display units could be arranged so that stocking is done from the rear of the units and food is then accurately sold in proper rotation. All these features would serve to improve the quality of food available to the consumer. This is technologically the best way to market fresh food to great numbers of people, and some aspects of this method of distribution are in use in some places.

However, we cannot necessarily expect change to continue unhampered by reaction. There are signs that cost-conscious consumers in the USA and Europe are turning away from the more expensive pre-prepared foods and concentrating on basic ingredients, in which they then want very good quality. It could be that in order to keep operating costs down shops will ultimately stock a simplified range of foodstuffs. Then the emphasis could be on quality, particularly in terms of flavour, which has been neglected in some foods.

There seems to have been some loss of confidence in pre-packed fruit and vegetables, so 'weigh and pay' areas for unwrapped produce are likely to be a feature of many supermarkets. Similarly many shops have found that the sight of real live butchers and bakers at work boosts the sales of meat and bread.

There may also in the future be more restrictions on the building of supermarkets in towns. This would result in the development of more out-of-town shopping areas, and in towns more chains of shops specializing in products of one type (meat, fish, bread or fruit, for example).

WHERE WILL CHANGE BE GREATEST?

Whatever future trends develop in food the greatest changes are likely to be in what is processed rather than in fresh produce, because in any industry innovation is highly esteemed. In the fresh produce context I think we can include straightforward frozen foods like uncoated fish fillets, chickens, vegetables and fruit. We can well think of these as 'quick-frozen long-life fresh foods', because the nature of food is so little changed by freezing. In the processed foods context I am particularly thinking of the many cases where part of the kitchen work has been done for us; the batter on the fish, the ready-made pies, the cakes, puddings, sauces, jams, icecreams and exotic savoury dishes. Here the range of possibilities is limitless; there are all the cuisines of the world to prepare and package before the 'new product' designers run out of ideas.

FOOD IS TO ENJOY

The great variety of food is one of the wonders of nature. Each homecoming from a shopping excursion can be the occasion for a small harvest festival, as the kitchen table is filled with purchases of breads, cheese, eggs, fruit and vegetables in all their beautiful shapes, colours and flavours. Food has been celebrated in 'still life' pictures the world over. A family can enjoy the beauty of natural foodstuffs and be thankful that in the Western world the choice of food is so wide. It is time to stop grumbling about minor changes and restrictions, and to do all we can to make sure that the best of basic foods hold places of high regard in the Food Choice Jungle of the future.

Suggestions for Further Reading

Burkitt, D. P. and Trowell, H. C. (editors), *Refined Carbohydrate Foods and Disease* (Academic Press, 1976).

Davidson, S., Passmore, R., Brock, J. F. and Truswell, A. S., *Human Nutrition and Dietetics* (Churchill Livingstone, 1975).

Fox, B. and Cameron, A. G., *Food Science* (University of London Press, 1970).

Gail Duff's Vegetarian Cookbook (Pan Books, 1979).

Green, Henrietta, *Fine-Flavoured Food: A Fresh Approach to Lighter Cookery* (Faber, 1978).

Ministry of Agriculture, Fisheries and Food, *Manual of Nutrition* (H.M.S.O., 1976).

Nilson, B., *Cooking for Special Diets* (Penguin Books, 2nd edition 1971).

Pyke, M., *Success in Nutrition* (John Murray, 1975).

Recommended Intakes of Nutrients for the United Kingdom (1969) (H.M.S.O., 1973).

Schroeder, H. A., *Trace Elements in Nutrition* (Faber, 1973).

Stanway, A., *Taking the Rough with the Smooth* (Pan, 1976).

Tannahill, R. *Food in History* (Paladin, 1975).

Trum Hunter, B., *The Natural Foods Cookbook* (Faber, 1975).

Tudge, C., *The Famine Business* (Faber, 1977).

For Children:
Newman, Nanette, *The Fun Food Factory* (G. Whizzard/André Deutsch, 1976).

Index

Fat(s)—cont.
  cooking, 26, 71, 86
  eating less, 74–6
  mono-unsaturated, 29, 71–2
  poly-unsaturated, 29, 71–2
  saturated, 29, 71–2
  types of and food containing,
    71–2
Feedstuffs, 186, 188
Fibre (cellulose), 20, 54, 58–65,
    81–2, 176, 178
Figs, 57, 98, 103
  fresh, 90
Fish, 26, 30, 36, 40, 44, 71, 76–7,
    82, 94, 96, 99, 105, 112,
    131–2, 164, 186
  canned, 97
  farming, 186
  fingers, 69, 85, 87
  oils, 71
  shell, 49
  white, 49, 69, 85, 87, 103
Fishing, future, 187
Flexifood, 159, 161
Flexitime, 159
Flour, 142–4
  products, 40, 60
  wheatmeal, 142
  wholemeal, 51, 65, 130, 142
Fluorine, 99
Folic acid, 96
Food
  convenience, 191
  distribution, 193–4
  frozen, 152–4, 187, 194
  growing, 156–8
  processing, 187, 189, 193
  scientists, 192
  vegetarian, 74, 75
Fruit, 28, 30, 65, 76–7, 96, 106,
    115, 163, 190–1
  canned, 90
  citrus, 148
  dried, 57, 65, 90, 114, 130
  fresh, 146–51

juices, 99, 130, 182, 184

Gall bladder, 172
Gall stones, 59, 61
Goals, dietary, 28–30
Gooseberries, 90, 105
Gout, 173
Grains, 23, 30, 40–1, 54–6, 76–7,
    165; see also Cereal(s)
  wholegrain foods, 82, 190
Grapefruit, 86, 105, 146–7
Grapes, 90
Greengages, 90
Growing food, 156–8

Haemorrhoids, 59, 60
Hake, 132
Ham, 69, 87, 95, 104
Hamburgers, 134
Harvesters, 191
Heart (meat), 76, 77
Heart disease, 58
Herrings, 48, 68–9, 85, 87, 103–4
Honey, 58
Huss (rock salmon), 132
Hydrogen, 97
Hypertension, 73

Icecream, 69, 86, 113
Iodine, 99
Iron, 20, 98, 100–3
Isoleucine, 39, 40

Jam, 58, 65
  conserves, 67
Joule, see Calories

Kidney, 77, 87, 94–6, 98, 112
Kilocalorie, see Calories
Kilojoule, see Calories

Lamb, 49, 69, 77, 102, 112
Lard, 71, 86
Leeks, 88
Legumes (pulses), 40, 41